1700 IN 70

1700 in 70

A WALK FOR A CAUSE

GITA BALAKRISHNAN

RUPA

Published by
Rupa Publications India Pvt. Ltd 2024
7/16, Ansari Road, Daryaganj
New Delhi 110002

Sales centres:
Bengaluru Chennai Hyderabad
Jaipur Kathmandu Kolkata
Mumbai Prayagraj

Copyright © Gita Balakrishnan 2024
Photos copyright © Gita Balakrishnan
Foreword copyright © Leander Paes 2024

P-ISBN: 978-93-6156-714-8
E-ISBN: 978-93-6156-633-2

First impression 2024

10 9 8 7 6 5 4 3 2 1

To Bala
Hand in hand, we walk into the twilight

To Pranav, Gaurav and Shreya
Your belief in me is my strength

To the Ethos Family
For walking the talk

CONTENTS

FOREWORD

Tennis, walking and architecture. What, if anything, do they share in common? Penning the foreword for this exceptional memoir by Gita, I can't keep from drawing parallels between her 1,700-kilometre journey on foot and my own experiences on the tennis court. I was intrigued by the idea of such an endeavour and went on to read more about it. There are many similarities and yet, the stories are distinct, each a testament to the unshakeable spirit that drives us. Playing tennis is healing and therapeutic to me, as long-distance walking is to Gita. Both demand willpower, discipline, focus, unwavering commitment and an undying passion to push one's boundaries. Gita champions the three essentials in life, which are mental, emotional and physical fitness.

Reading about Gita's encounters with people, environments, nature and much more along the not-so-traversed parts of this country, I recalled the numerous learnings from my own travels—every match, every opponent, every doubles partnership and everyone I crossed paths with.

Architecture and buildings are an integral element of our lives as we spend a significant part of it in enclosed spaces. Yet, a common notion exists that design is a luxury reserved for a select few. Gita's mission to explore the power of design and to build awareness about people's problems through this unique and imaginative 'vehicle' of walking is one-of-a-kind. I've had the privilege of using my platform as an athlete to support various causes and fundraisers, and I've witnessed the incredible impact that individuals can make when they combine their passion with a purpose. Gita's 'Walk for Arcause' resonates deeply with me as it blends a physically arduous task with a social cause close to one's heart. Gita empowers people along her journey to dream big and gives them the courage to achieve their dreams.

Kolkata, the city where this remarkable journey began, is my birthplace and holds a special corner in my heart.

Vigour and focus are paramount in any expedition, be it on the tennis court or the long road. As athletes, we are well aware of the importance of keeping our bodies in the best shape. Staying fit is not just a choice but a way of life—an investment for our profession. Throughout my career, I faced my share of health setbacks, from injuries to surgeries. It was the unflinching belief in my abilities and the determination to overcome that saw me through. I read with familiarity the health issues Gita encountered along her way and about the challenging accident in Gwalior that placed the completion of the walk in jeopardy. Her resilience and determination, similar to that of many in the sports arena, propelled her forward, and she emerged stronger than ever, something we can all learn from. Our truth!

At the peak of our careers, we athletes are busy chasing our glory on the grandest of stages. However, when the limelight fades and the racquets are hung up, we must come to terms with the routine of normal life. Spanning 70 days of relentless walking, *1700 in 70* also mirrors the challenge of returning to the routine of everyday existence after an exceptionally transformative expedition. It is a recount of a journey from the extraordinary, back to the ordinary— filled with vivid memories. The thirst for more has pushed her to not stop at one but embark upon a series of 'quests' to experience the country's rich tapestry—learning and sharing on the go. She has already accomplished a journey across the borders—all the way to Dhaka from Kolkata—on a similar mission, a glimpse of which can also be seen in this book. I am only eager to know what lies ahead for her.

As I read through the pages of *1700 in 70*, I felt like I was walking alongside Gita, experiencing my country's landscapes, cultures and challenges through her eyes. I urge you to take this journey with her to discover the transformative potential of design and be inspired by one woman's incredible determination to make a difference. With each step she took, Gita Balakrishnan walked not just for herself but for a greater purpose—that of collective action to create goodness in our world. And I am with Gita on her life's mission.

Gita's journey is a testimony to the extraordinary potential within each of us to bring about change, and I am honoured to introduce you to her spectacular story and why she is 'My Champ'!

—Leander Paes
Professional Tennis Player and Motivational Speaker

INTRODUCTION

I underwent four surgeries—two major and two minor—between the ages of twenty-two and twenty-eight. I had contracted tuberculosis and went through a regimen of treatments as I reached thirty. By the time I was thirty-eight, many doctors advised a total hysterectomy. My eyes often turned red as a symptom of an autoimmune disorder. When I turned forty, I was diagnosed with seronegative rheumatoid arthritis (seronegative RA) and was on medication for over four years. The seronegative RA manifested in different ways; I could be bent over in pain with a bad back or could not walk because of bursitis in an ankle or tendonitis in different joints. My body was fairly battered with these ailments and I regularly wondered about what life held in store for me. I was undergoing extreme stress at work as well.

I had only heard about people being transformed by physical activity until I got to experience it. With a physical activity regimen, I was able to pick myself up and get well enough to successfully complete a 1,700-kilometre cross-country quest on foot.

This piece of non-fiction is a personal account of physical endurance and the spiritual growth I experienced during an incredible journey of 1,700 km over 70 days. I believe that this story can be aspirational as it is a tale of someone who found solace by taking to running at the age of forty-five and then went on to complete an epic 1,700-kilometre journey from Kolkata to Delhi on foot at fifty-three! Menopause is a time in life when people slow down, and here I was, pressing on the accelerator.

The Oxford Dictionary defines a quest[1] as 'a long search for something, especially for some quality, such as happiness,' but when I set out in February 2022, I knew that my journey had not been undertaken in search of a singular 'quality'. This book, then, is about

---

[1] *Oxford Learner's Dictionaries*, https://www.oxfordlearnersdictionaries.com/definition/english/quest_1?q=quest. Accessed on 22 November 2023.

my own definition of a quest. It is about how I wove two disparate loves together to pursue a quest that made for a meaningful life ahead. It is about a quest to view my vocation through the billion lenses of our country.

I am an architect. I have often heard people casually mixing up the words 'architect' and 'architecture'. Architects are often heard lamenting the state of the profession while others do not even know of architects. This is ironic as we all are constantly interacting with buildings and spaces—designed or otherwise—at almost every single moment of our lives. A shelter is considered a basic necessity for human beings, which is exemplified in the famous slogan, *roti, kapda aur makaan* (food, clothing and shelter). In our country, it is not too common to seek professional support for design as a service; architecture and design professionals do not get what they deserve, nor are architects and designers looked upon as essential service providers.

My walk was designed to serve a major purpose: to throw light upon the power of design—something grossly undervalued by the common people, the government and society at large. Design is an integral part of our everyday lives. Yet, in common knowledge, it is classified as a luxury. Most people do not seek this power for themselves or their habitat. And those who need it desperately cannot afford it. On this walk, many opportunities presented themselves. I could identify the grievances of the common people through my interactions with communities in villages, towns and cities along the way, and I subsequently picked out actionable areas upon which designers could work. The Walk was about the power of design, but *1700 in 70* is about the walk, about my journey. Nonetheless, as it has been drafted on the table of an architect, there are many references to our habitat and the changes that can be brought through empathy and design. This book also tells stories about the struggles and challenges of modernizing the rural without urbanizing it. Therefore, the overall intent of 'Walk for Arcause' (as this walk and campaign are titled) was to draw attention to the architects working in the social realm and to make architectural social responsibility an area that needs to become a serious topic of conversation and action within the architectural community. While the walk helped identify some important differences that architects and designers have made in society, more importantly, I realized the difference they still need to make in the different spheres of life.

1700 in 70 is a narrative describing the beauty of the diverse experiences that our country has to offer. India measures 3,214 km from the north to the south and 2,933 km from the east to the west.[2] She is divided into the following climatic zones: alpine, humid subtropical, tropical wet-dry, tropical wet, semi-arid, arid and composite. The climate and the available natural resources in a particular region determine the kind of crops that can be cultivated and animals that can be reared, which are directly related to the cuisine, the clothes people wear and the kind of homes they build. The vastness of our land ensures and endures with magical ease a variety of social, cultural, environmental and natural experiences, to say the least. I started my journey in the tropical wet-dry region of West Bengal and walked largely through the humid subtropical climatic zones of Jharkhand, Madhya Pradesh and Uttar Pradesh while skimming over a bit of arid Rajasthan to reach the semi-arid Haryana and Delhi. There were days when I encountered six different dialects over a distance of just 20 km!

Contained here are stories of an India I observed closely. Acts of kindness nudged me on. Here, I share stories of people who had little to subsist on but a lot to give—the stories of inspiration. I hope that my experiences of traversing the known, unknown, busy and calm stretches of my country; my interactions at the heart, hinterlands and peripheral settlements; will be a guide for a moderately new traveller to India, as well as a great resource for those who know this country well. I hope that this book will pique the curiosity of teachers and learners to explore new ways of teaching and learning outside the classroom. While formal education happens in the confines of schools and colleges, learning continues only when we keep engaging with all that is around us. We need to develop skills to actively learn and complement our institutional education so that we can craft our own paths and personalities.

---

[2]Know India, India at a Glance, Government of India, https://knowindia.india.gov. in/profile/india-at-a-glance.php Accessed on 22 November 2023.

1700 in 70 is a memoir, and it includes anecdotes of people I met en route, choices I made along the way and my engagement with the changing natural, built, social, political and cultural landscape. I have dedicated at least one chapter to each state that I have traversed. I keenly observed how one state amalgamated with the next and how they were culturally, socially and politically different from each other. The walk and the journey are referred to as 'the 1700'. Most chapters are titled according to the days—with the first day labelled 'Day 1'. There are many remarkable places, people and organizations that I engaged with along the way. Some stood out, and I have labelled them as 'showstoppers' and have also provided a short account of why they impressed me and caught my eye.

When people learn about this walk, many questions come flying at me. How many kilometres were covered in a day? What did you eat? Did you feel unsafe? What were your best and worst experiences? Why? How? *1700 in 70* attempts to satiate many such curiosities. Readers will find insights into the incubation of the idea, planning and how the journey becomes a fountainhead for future plans, as well as a few accounts and incidents of my life that make me who I am: a go-getter, a meticulous planner and an aggregator of goodwill—all of which I harnessed to make this dream of a lifetime come true. The final section of this book also recounts the walk that followed: 306 km in 17 days, from Kolkata to Dhaka—a very different experience from the first long walk.

My life has not been an ordinary one. I was raped and almost murdered at sixteen. I survived this assault and I am grateful for each day that I get to live. Would I have had the courage and the gumption to attempt this 1,700 km feat if not for the strength that I had acquired in the horrific incident's aftermath? We shall never know. But my survival has certainly defined me and helped me become who I am today. And conclusively, even if I say so myself, this book also describes a journey of physical and mental strength and is dedicated to all those who avidly follow physical and mental well-being and to those who have just begun their walk down that path. Additionally, it serves people looking for accounts of self-awareness, mindfulness and an alternate way of living life.

Born out of personal experiences, my narrative is a real story—an in-depth account of the processes of self-awareness, self-discovery and perseverance, in light of being questioned by myself as well as others. This work is an exercise drenched in careful contemplation and revelation. *1700 in 70* is for those who live life as a quest.

Walk,
and you shall seek.
Walk,
and you shall find.
Walk,
and you shall give.
Walk,
and you shall receive.
Walk,
and you shall reach.

CHAPTER 1

THE BEGINNING OF
THE REST OF MY LIFE

Day 70
23 April 2022

'When you walk, you arrive with every step.'

—THICH NHAT HANH

I lay awake last night in anticipation. Today was to be the final lap in a long and arduous—but fulfilling—journey. I was on the cusp of making history. A 1,700-kilometre walk from Kolkata to Delhi is something not many can boast about. And yet, I felt no excitement or even relief. There was only a feeling of calm. A sense of purpose to complete what had been started.

70 days
25,72,420 steps
849 villages, towns and cities
6 states and 1 National Capital Territory
Scores of people, smiles and interactions
Immeasurable joy.

∽

Day 71
24 April 2022

A symbolic walk, from Raj Ghat to Red Fort, commemorating India's 75th year of Independence, marked the culmination of the first-ever 'Walk for Arcause'. I chose Raj Ghat in order to recall the spirit of

Mahatma Gandhi's Dandi March in 1930, 92 years earlier, when he and 78 satyagrahis walked in protest against a tax on salt. On this last stretch of my humble journey, people from different walks of life, belonging to a diverse age group that included a good number of architects, came together to reinforce the intent of the walk. This beautiful and fulfilling journey, all along its length, gave us great insights into our world and the role designers can collectively assume to make it better.

And just like that, it was over. The breathtaking sunrises in different landscapes each day, the smiles of people that melted my heart, the vivid colours of our incredible country and many more such images flashed through my mind. No, this was not the end. In fact, this was just the beginning!

A walk in the park, it was not.
Calluses and blisters do not grow in parks;
they grow on feet in duress.
Pain, suffering, inequities
are not what you see in a park.
Children running barefoot to schools,
not that either.

Unending roads with no trees,
sweltering heat and rare spots to rest,
and no pretty waterbodies with benches around.
No candy man, no swans in the lake.
No, a walk in the park, it was not.

But wait.

A walk in the park, it was!
Surreal sunrises that heal the heart,
colours of nature that touch the soul,
cheerful grins and unfeigned salutations,
and unknown people were mine.

Hearths of the earth,
crafts of the soil,
celebrations of a place,

stories of our land,
visions of tomorrow,
which together we make
into sounds of our cause

Yes, a walk in the park, it was.

CHAPTER 2

WHAT WAS IT LIKE?

'*What was it like?*' This was the question on the lips of everyone I met once the walk concluded—at talks, on walks, at parties, everywhere! I froze every time I heard it, not quite knowing how to answer. Words such as 'fantastic', 'incredible', 'unbelievable' and 'amazing' all pale in comparison when describing an experience like this. How can a word, a phrase, a sentence or even a paragraph portray a journey of a lifetime? The intricacies, challenges, joys, fears, loneliness, explorations and discoveries of 70 long days?

Our wonderful country unfolded in front of me with each step I took, and the pace was gentle enough to allow India's magnitude and diversity to sink in. I encountered different lifestyles among the people that I met almost every day. The variety of architectural styles, landscapes, crafts, art, culinary preferences, colours, attires, fabrics, crops, occupations, dialects, customs and faiths unravelled in front of my eyes, like a montage. I marvelled at the peaceful coexistence of these different, and often conflicting, pieces of the 'Indian' mosaic.

Buddhist philosophy refers to *shunyata* (or the voidness) as the ultimate reality. Is there an apparent conflict in the statement? The contents of Thich Nhat Hahn's *No Mud No Lotus*[1] rang true as I experienced extreme hardships to feel the joys of this journey. Solitude was mine, and so was loneliness. While I walked alone, I felt one with the many whose paths crossed mine. The daily physical stress helped me value the few hours of rest that I got. The anxiousness I sometimes felt at the end of my day's walk turned into peace as the early mornings dawned with sheer bliss. The silent mornings made the

---

[1]Nhat Hanh, Thich, *No Mud, No Lotus: The Art of Transforming Suffering*, Parallax Press, Berkeley, CA, 7 December 2014.

sound of the birds, peacocks and the morning ragas along the way so much more melodious. The darkness before daybreak brought to life the colours of the firmament to spark a special beginning to every day. I walked alone believing in the power of the collective.

I saw an India that was content. I expected to be scorched by tales of poverty, and while the many people I met did recount and share their miseries and problems, they would end their outpourings by saying, '*Hum santusht hai*. (Nonetheless, we are satisfied.)' While I was walking and connecting with their woes, I was reminded of the kings of yore who would walk through their kingdoms in disguise to understand what people thought of their rule. If politicians and those in government and governance could make a similar effort to feel the pulse of the people they are supposed to be serving today, the impact of their actions would be meaningful and direct. They would also be transformed to discover and take the right path. Having their ears on the ground would help in growing their political and bureaucratic careers as well.

Gradually, acceptance became my strongest ally as I navigated the ups and downs that this trip held in store for me. Losing my way meant walking more, and this can be particularly harrowing and demotivating when one has many miles to clock each day. But the joy of discovery that unfolded on such detours made up for the exhaustion. Acceptance is also a tool for survival for many in our country, and it should not be construed as a weak trait. Nilmuni Murmu's life exemplifies the fact that acceptance often begets great strength.

Showstopper 1

Originally from Lalgarh, Jhargram, in the heart of Jangal Mahal, Nilmuni is a widow who lives life on her own terms. Although she lives alone on the fringes of Uchi Geri, a hamlet in West Bengal, she appears to be the spokesperson for all villagers. Despite her diminutive personality, she commands huge respect.

Another pattern I observed was how awareness, whether limited or heightened, aided people to accept their situations and aspirations. Technology, the internet and social media have penetrated the remotest corners of our country, thereby changing trends, preferences and ambitions. Although everyone may not have access to them, the sway that local influencers wield is evident.

Despite the influx of an urban way of life and subsequent modernization, the rustic charm of the rural and small-town lives has not yet been completely eroded. Simplicity ensures the blurring of barriers, and it helps people bond as a community. Empathy for each other and the environment is the bedrock of their way of living.

The power of a smile (and the universality of this power) is something I witnessed at almost every moment I walked. A smile led to the exchange of a wave, a word, a chat and often a story. I made the stories of Surbala, Sujit, Ghorai, Jasodha, Ram Lakhan and Lakhan Srivastav a part of my story. And as I walked along, leaving them behind, I wondered if our paths would ever cross again. As Sujit grew to be a young man, would he retain the curiosity and the zest that I had sensed in his questions? Would Jasodha live to be a hundred years old? Would Surbala's daughter Malati pursue her career or end up getting married to lead a life like her mother's? Would Lakhan Srivastav secure the government job that he so desperately sought? Would Anjali build the home of her dreams? Would they remember me and our interactions as they move on with their lives?

CHAPTER 3

I HAD A DREAM

194 Days Before the Flag-off

I *have a treasure cache of dreams into which I reach from time to time; some treasures I cultivate and some I hand out for others to breathe life into. There is also a secret pocket in this cache containing dreams rather dear to me. I often take them out, stroke them, explore them, nurture them and wait for them to come of age.*

A 1,700-kilometre journey on foot—why had I contemplated such a mammoth task? The very thought gives me an adrenaline rush.

But I had started this not because of the rush and thrill. Physical, intellectual and emotional challenges are the reasons that made me dig deep into my repositories and discover the toughness I never believed I had. Many incidents have made me who I am—whether it be the first-ever quiz on architecture, the first-ever online learning portal for design and architecture in the country or taking up running at the age of forty-five and graduating to full marathons—these challenges continue to be the reason for my being and my becoming.

I had been running three days a week for close to seven years. On 13 November 2021, I switched to walking. A lot changed. I did not draw as many stares, smiles and nods of respect now that I was walking like so many others. The sight of a salt-and-pepper-haired woman running intensely had earlier brought a fair share of admirers. Walking has taught me patience and continues to do so. I need to be on my feet for twice as long to cover the same distance. Running is meditative for me while walking can be distracting. When running, putting one foot in front of the other grounds me. Walking, on the other hand, makes me see things around me, gives me time to observe and slows me down. These distractions work the same magic to hook me to the present. So walking is meditative too in its own way.

The desire to undertake a long-distance cross-country walk had been brewing in me for a few years. It was spawned by an article that I read in a newspaper in 2018 about the Peace March of 1987,[2] an initiative under which Priya Dutt walked from Mumbai to Amritsar with her father, Sunil Dutt. I could imagine the different moments and experiences that had transformed both of them during this journey.

Recently, when the pandemic struck, I followed the heart-rending stories of thousands of migrant workers who were forced to walk back from a life they had dreamed for themselves. Images of a solitary slipper, spilt food or a doll on the road were grim reminders of the life they had left behind. Their long walk must have changed them as their lives were upended. I often imagine the conversations they may have had to keep their spirits high as they undertook this extremely challenging trip. Did they hum a tune? Did they notice the flowing river? How did they find the strength and resolve to comfort others and offer help when being in deep distress? This exodus was a lesson in empathy and responsibility for all humankind. It is ironic though—I speak of building endurance; I had an elaborate plan for my walk and I treated it as an adventure. But for them it was an ordeal.

However, this very irony spurred me on. I decided to use my journey to touch lives and make a difference. As an architect with a reasonably large network of designers, professionals, academics and students, I aimed to leverage this network into making a collaborative effort to examine the role design and designers can play in impacting lives. This walk was meant to goad the members of my professional community to weave social responsibility into their practice and to not lose sight of social, cultural and environmental justice. My intent was also to shine a spotlight on the role of the designer and the architect, professionals whose professions are largely unknown in common society.

Hence, in July 2021, I committed to the Walk for Arcause. I told

[2]Nichola, 'Remembering Sunil Dutt: He had Walked from Mumbai to Amritsar for Peace', *Peepingmoon.com*, Clapping Hands Private Limited, 6 June 2018, https://www.peepingmoon.com/entertainment-news/news/16659/Remembering-Sunil-Dutt-He-had-walked-from-Mumbai-to-Amritsar-for-peace.html. Accessed on 22 November 2023.

my husband Bala and my mother of my plans at the dining table over a weekend lunch. Bala has always encouraged me in all my endeavours and he did not hesitate to do so again once he heard my proposal. My mother assumed I was joking at first and she quipped that she would run alongside me. But once she read the determined look on my face, she silently spurred me on. Then it was time to tell the children. We set up a video call where I broke the news to Pranav and Gaurav, our two sons, and to Shreya, Pranav's wife who had just joined our family. While their expressions spelt disbelief—'Here we go again on a rollercoaster,' they seemed to say—it was also clear that they were going to join me in my excitement.

There were four confidantes with whom I shared the idea: my cousin Major General Dharmarajan, who has had a penchant for adventure all his life; K. Shravan, a young friend; Rajiv Ahir, a dear batchmate from my days at architecture school who went on to become an IPS officer; and Hermanprit Singh, another close friend and IPS officer. Dharmarajan and Shravan prodded me further and were very excited about the possibilities. Herman, at that point, was sceptical and evidently did not think of it as a great idea. Rajiv heard me out and sent me back to the drawing table, telling me that I needed a robust plan if I wanted to be taken seriously.

And off I went back to the table. The next couple of months were spent thinking, researching, planning, writing and estimating the journey. Initially, I contemplated setting out in October to complete the walk before the New Year. Reconnaissance revealed the list of tasks: getting a team together, raising funds, planning a social media campaign and creating content in the form of presentations and flash cards for formal and informal interactions with people in different locations. Reviewing the quantum of work for a well-oiled campaign, I finally decided upon February as the flag-off month, and we zeroed in on 13 February as the date. This gave me enough time to complete my other work-related commitments and focus on the task at hand—enjoying the journey of my lifetime.

The pandemic was still raging in December. January brought its new variant, Omicron, and I kept hoping that it would ebb away by the time I set out. I contracted COVID on 5 January, and my training was affected until I came out of isolation on the 13th, after testing negative. I attempted to keep walking inside the four walls of my room during these eight days and managed to clock up to 16,000 steps on most days. This had my husband quipping that even a caged lion would not pace the way I was pacing. Even though the pandemic was a blip in my training, everything worked out fine.

Once I had committed to the walk, my mind was abuzz with ideas on how my love for walking/running could come together with my passion for bridging the gap between the design community and other communities at large. I nostalgically looked back at my own trajectory that had brought me to this point.

CHAPTER 4

WHAT MAKES ME!

13,511 Days Before the Flag-off

Something happened to me on my way to heaven, thirty-seven years ago, but once I had reached the gates, I was sent back to live a fulfilling life for a while longer!

And it has turned out to be quite a life!

I do not wish to dwell on the circumstances of that night and will confine myself to say that every time I hear the word 'rape' and the phrase 'left to die', words often used these days while reporting such incidents, I travel back to a lifetime ago when I was merely sixteen-years-old.

I wrote this on 27 February 1986, a little over a year after the incident.

It's been over a year,
but it could have been yesterday
when God decided
I was no more to stay
in this wonderful land of His,
which I would so terribly miss.

And so, on the night of 7th February,
after I went to bed very weary,
I felt hands throttling me—
who they belonged to, I could hardly see—
for the curtains were drawn
and the lights were not on.

For help, I shouted!
And hurt me, he did!

He threw me on the floor
and hurt me even more.
Upon my throat I felt extreme pressure—
the agony is hard to describe in any measure.
My head felt like lead,
and I was as good as dead.

But no, I decided to fight!
And God decided that wasn't the night.
He gave me the strength and willpower
And I bore all without an utter.
I pretended to be dead
where I lay beside my bed,
the man thought he had completed his task,
and walked away after taking off his mask.

And that is how I am writing this today.

Yes, there was an attempt on my life. Thinking I was dead, a monster raped me. I had to scale two compound walls to get to my neighbour's house and raise an alarm. My father chased the case in court for twelve long years to get a conviction for attempted murder and rape, and by that time, I had already delivered my first son. While we were advised not to file a rape case, I insisted that we should, believing that it would help in putting a stop to such horrifying incidents instead of only hoping that they will never happen again. The decision came quite naturally to me, but it was considered a bold one. The man was released on bail merely two weeks after he had been arrested.

While writing this, I have been trying to recollect my feelings. Strangely, I am not able to recall the sort of fear that could have stopped me from doing the right thing. Not that I did not break into cold sweats in the middle of the night or swoon during a movie at a theatre; those were involuntary reactions of me succumbing to my fears.

I retain a vivid memory of my first day in court. Even now I am unable to explain my actions on that day. I chose to dress carefully so that I appeared good and happy. We were seated in the first row; the beast was in the last row. I remember standing up, turning around and looking him squarely in the eye—that was my moment of release.

The later hearings were held in camera, in the privacy of the judge's chambers.

I remember asking myself often—'Why me?'—and answering myself too—'If not me, it would have been someone else, and I was picked because I had the inner strength to endure and the wisdom to find meaning in what happened to me.' Can meaning really be found in brutality? Can any sense be made out of it? Maybe not, but that is one way of dealing with the bizarre. I thank the high heavens each day for the way I emerged from this experience—stronger, without feeling guilty, angry, frustrated or depressed enough to ruin the rest of my life the way many beautiful lives have been ruined and are being ruined as you are reading this. I believe that because I was meant to live another day, every day is a bonus and I treasure each moment, realizing that I was meant to live for a purpose.

I try to find that purpose in all that I do. I ask myself, 'Am I doing enough?'

As a parent today, I sometimes relive the horror and anguish of my parents. But then I focus on what 'is' rather than what could have been. My parents did have the joy of getting me married and they did revel in the delight of seeing their grandchildren grow into young men. Yes, I did get married and happily. There were many who advised me against telling my story to my future husband. My response was simple. I am proud of the way I dealt with the incident, and if someone who is going to be an important part of my life cannot accept me for who I am, then he does not deserve to be in my life. I was pleasantly surprised when I found out that my honesty was the first thing that my husband liked about me.

I studied architecture at the School of Planning and Architecture in Delhi in 1985–90. I was probably the only person from my college who pursued and opted to complete the stipulated six-month practical training outside India at that time. I went to the Centre for Building Performance and Diagnostics at Carnegie Mellon University in Pittsburgh. It was not common in those days. My perseverance to carve out and secure this huge opportunity was one of the first battles I won on many fronts. I remember why it mattered to me so much. I needed to follow my dreams with a passion because I was so close to not having any at all. You value what you have the most only when you are without all of it, even if it is just for a moment.

I am now at a stage in life where what happened in the past is a distant but vivid memory. My voice does not quiver when I narrate my story, but I am moved by what I read and see around me and feel helpless during such times. I think there is something to learn from my story and from the stories of many others who deal so well with the cards handed out to them by life that rarely is everything lost. However, I was fortunate to have understanding parents and thoughtful friends who stood by me like rocks. Most of all, I found a life partner who helped me overcome the grief and the fear that was present in many layers and many forms, who knew when to stay silent and when to say a comforting word. Hence, it is the blessings that I count and not the misfortunes. I chose a path not taken by many in my professional and personal life, and I am comfortable where I am today.

One does not need a trauma of this magnitude at such a tender age to be able to chart a specific and meaningful course in life. I could have been the person I am today even without it. I do ponder over whether I would have been different without this experience. Would I have followed the much-trodden path, not discovering the excitement that I now do each day? Would I have not felt the impatience that I do every moment of my new lease of life? Would I have not dreamed up a special life and lived my special dreams?

I am a happy woman.

I am a reasonably good wife to a great husband and a nagging mom to my two boys and daughter-in-law.

I am—and this I say with confidence—a good human being.

I am a restless professional waiting to live my next dream.

I am all this and more, despite what happened to me.

Yes, something did happen on my way to heaven the first time around, and I hope nothing happens on my second voyage—whenever that might be. A lot has happened and continues to happen in between the two upward journeys and I would like to treasure those as memories of a life well-lived.

Top: *Flagged off by construction workers Prashanta Naskar and Vijay Sharma from Victoria Memorial in Kolkata*

Bottom: *Day 1—Walking over the Howrah Bridge in Kolkata*

Top: *Day 3—With students of Arambagh Vivekananda Academy post a 'Design as a Career' session at Arambagh in West Bengal*

Bottom: *Day 6—Interacting with women from a self-help group—organized by the NGO Mallabhum Prayas—at Madhabpur in West Bengal*

Top: *Interacting with Nilmuni Murmu at Uchi Geri, a hamlet in West Bengal*
Bottom: *(Left) Stretching post-walk in West Bengal*
(Right) En route from Bankura to Purulia in West Bengal

Top: *Interacting with the locals on common building practices at Kotulpur in West Bengal*
Bottom: *Day 11—A selfie with the locals near Jhalda in West Bengal*

Top: *Day 16—Dancing with local girls at ASHA, an NGO based at Ranchi in Jharkhand*
Bottom: *Sumari, a brick kiln worker's daughter, who wishes to pursue a career in geography*

Top: *Day 18—With students of St Joseph's Rural Community College at Chandwa in Jharkhand*
Bottom: *Day 20—Felt like going to school with the children at Nadbelwa in Jharkhand*

Top: *Day 24—With Sunita Devi, a Rani Mistry (master trainer in masonry), at Latehar in Jharkhand*
Bottom: *Interacting with the locals at Palamu in Jharkhand*

Walking through Garhwa in Jharkhand

CHAPTER 5

I COULD HAVE BEEN QUEEN!

19,541 Days Before the Flag-off
27 July 1968

Kolkata in 1968 was a different place. It was Calcutta, a city where Pam Crain and Usha Uthup crooned and had their audience swaying; a city that barely missed becoming the national capital after Independence because the British Empire decided to move the capital to Delhi in 1911. The streets of Calcutta were washed every day and every building whispered the story of its making. Calcutta of the '60s thrived on its rich legacy of freedom fighters, philosophers, intellectuals, writers and artists. The late '60s were witness to the fallout of the culture of protests and strikes, eventually leading to many factories and manufacturing industries moving out of the state of West Bengal. Power cuts, or 'load-shedding' as it is locally called, became a norm. It was during one such power cut that I announced my arrival. My mother had to walk down five floors after her labour pains had started to get to the Union Nursing Home on Robinson Street. I was delivered there by Dr Chakravarthy.

A few years ago, before he passed away, my father told me that he had toyed with the idea of calling me *Rani* or even '*Queen*' since we lived in Queen's Mansion at that point in time. That is when I realized that there is a lot in a name; some paths choose you because your name is etched on them. But I was not to be Queen. My parents had attended some lectures on spirituality and Gita chose me. We left Calcutta soon after, and it is fortuitous that I returned with my husband and two sons thirty-three years later to the city. I lived here for the longest period of my life in one place, at Calcutta, now Kolkata. What is in a name? Kolkata is not Calcutta—the city I saw when I returned was a far cry from the one portrayed to me by my parents.

I spent most of my childhood in Hyderabad, then a sleepy little town. My schooling at St. Anne's High School, a convent in Vijayanagar Colony, is what probably made discipline and rigour a part of my character. Being the only daughter and the youngest of three siblings, I did get to have my way often. I was one of the first girls to cycle to school. Although a distance of a mere kilometre, a young girl cycling on the main roads was not a common sight in those days. When I visit Hyderabad and retrace the route now, the traffic makes me wonder whether any parent will be at peace with their child cycling on these roads today. As I walk over the gentle slope (which then seemed huge), I realize that those simple allowances that my parents gave me have allowed me to grow into who I am.

I may not have been born with a silver spoon but we lived a very comfortable life. Despite us never wanting anything, we never got more than we needed. I had no more than four to six good outfits at any point in time. We did go on long road trips to explore different parts of South India. Did *that* nurture my thirst for travel and exploration?

My father, an engineer by education and a chess and cricket enthusiast, had humble beginnings. He slowly worked his way up to give us a life where we certainly felt like we were better off than many. He placed education on a high pedestal and ensured that we got the best of it and also encouraged us to aspire. My father had a head full of quotes and he would not shy away from using them. He displayed his wizardry in mathematics and numbers. My mother, on the other hand, was Mumbai-bred. It still breaks my heart that she had to give up her medical education after a year as she got married. While she was given the freedom to make the choice between marriage and education, as the eldest of six children, she felt that marriage was the right decision at that time. Having lost the opportunity, getting a good education was of utmost importance in her view as well. So my brothers ended up completing their engineering at IIT Madras and Kanpur while I went on to study architecture at the School of Planning and Architecture (SPA) in Delhi.

Moving to Delhi just before the 1982 Asian Games came as a

huge culture shock. I was accepted in Class 10 at St. Mary's School, Safdarjung Enclave, and had to cope with a lot. The shift from a simple Andhra Pradesh state board to CBSE in the year I was to give my All India Secondary School Examination proved to be a tough challenge. It took a few years to find my groove in this happening city, which was as different from Hyderabad as can be, from the people to the lifestyle, attitude and sheer scale. The rape and the attempted murder in this new city, New Delhi, shoved me out of my childhood and ushered in womanhood. My adolescence was so brutally curtailed that I hardly remember it. Yes, sixteen may be past adolescence for many, but I had my own milestones.

Architecture was not my first preference as a career but I was gently goaded to pursue it by my uncle, a civil engineer who worked on housing technologies specifically for rural India. Holidays in Chennai, then known as Madras, meant having conversations with him regarding what he was passionate about and some site visits too. The house he built for himself is an exhibition of all the ways different materials and technology could be deployed. What I saw and heard obviously made an impression on my young mind, and architecture did not seem as alien. Retrospectively, I recall bricks lying in our backyard in Hyderabad and how I would build walls a couple of feet high using the bricks and mud to make different rooms of a small make-believe home. Those games must have had their own influence over my choice of career too.

Ivan Lendl is known to have said, 'If I don't practise the way I should, then I won't play the way that I know I can.'[3] I am often asked if I am a practising architect. What I have chosen to do in all these years is certainly unconventional. I practise the way I do only because I believe I am doing what I am best at.

After my graduation in architecture, we moved to Bangalore, now Bengaluru. I was disillusioned with the job opportunities there and the conventional career paths for architecture graduates. I responded to an advertisement from the Association for Voluntary Action and

---

[3] ATP Heritage, 'Ivan Lendl: The Monk In The Iron Mask', *ATP Tour*, ATP Tour, Inc., 28 March 2020, https://www.atptour.com/en/news/atp-heritage-lendl-no-1-fedex-atp-rankings/. Accessed on 22 November 2023.

Services (AVAS), a non-profit, for the role of a creative educationist in slums. I joined them as a shelter coordinator because they fortunately needed one. Anita Reddy, the main force behind AVAS, had a profound impact on me with her never-ending zeal and unmatched conviction and commitment. Many years later, I proudly joined Anita as one of the trustees. In the early years, while my role was primarily that of an architect, the lines were blurred between being an architect and a social activist. I became a part of all the participatory processes that go into making such projects successful, specifically the community meetings that were held either at daybreak or after sunset. Terms such as 'participation', 'sustainability', 'social collateral' and 'empowerment' grew from being jargon to missions. I helped organize exercises wherein the slum-dwellers, prior to the redesign, were asked to draw their dream home. This brought up interesting aspects; the women would depict wells as a part of their house and the men drew shops or animal shelters.

It was around this time that I designed my first house, a project with a lot of constraints. The client (another Balakrishnan, incidentally) and I decided that we would try and lessen the burden on the environment. I have very fond memories of this house because I spent all my time on site, learning from those who build. I actually made some soil-cement blocks myself and even laid a few courses of masonry! This was a very exciting phase in my life. I chose to stay away from conventional architectural practice and decided to forge a path of my own. Why did I choose to do all these varied things that were not really the norm for an architect? I did so because I had to be comfortable with myself and for that, I would have to do things that I believed in. As Mark Twain once said, 'A man cannot be comfortable without his own approval.'[4]

This initial phase lasted around a decade, and the lessons I learned during this phase were extremely important in determining what I chose to do in the years that followed. I noticed and studied the wonderful efforts of various people in the field of construction and academics. Having experienced the feeling of inadequacy when I graduated, I felt

---

[4]Twain, Mark, *What Is Man? and Other Philosophical Writings,* The Iowa Center for Textual Studies, University of California Press, Berkeley, CA, 1973, 138.

the need to reach out and equip young minds to be agents of change, to lead and not just follow and to contribute positively and actively towards making a difference. Hence, I started Ethos in 2002 upon moving to Kolkata, the place of my birth. Ethos was conceptualized with the intention of bringing together students, professionals and industries in the built environment sector. Through this platform, budding professionals can empower and engage with each other. As one of the four verticals of Ethos, I introduced Ethos Foundation and Arcause as a platform for acknowledging, enlisting and actualizing the Social Responsibilities of Architects, Designers, Engineers and others associated with the Construction field (ACED community).

I am fortunate. I enjoyed what I did during my initial working years and did only what I enjoyed in the last two and a half decades or so. But during those early years, the path I ended up taking was more chance than choice, and I shudder to think I may have ended up elsewhere had the right choices not been made by chance. This is the need that I am trying to fulfil through Ethos—to build awareness among budding professionals so that they are able to make conscious choices and are aware of the world outside their institutions from the beginning of their graduate programs.

During this latter two-decade-long journey, I realized the role architecture and design can play in changing lives. Through our collaborations and work with the Saint Gobain Grants Program, I was introduced and moved by the thought-provoking solutions that Siddhant Shah proposed for the visually challenged to experience museums[5] and this eventually led to him setting up his NGO, Access for All. Aakriti Verma designed a prototype home for the flood-prone areas of Bihar[6] (which moved up and floated 12 feet above ground

---

[5]Rajesh, Anoushka. 'Making Art Accessible to the Visually Impaired: A Conversation with Siddhant Shah', *Art Fervour*, 3 December 2020, https://www.artfervour.com/making-art-accessible-to-the-visually-impaired-a-conversation-with-siddhant-shah/. Accessed on 22 November 2023.

[6]Verma, Aakriti, Buoyant Rural Household, 2012. National Institute of Technology, Raipur, graduation thesis.

level during floods). Aniket Risbud,[7] Rinky Haldar[8] and Avilash Bardhan are among many who turned their attention to making the lives of migrant workers comfortable. Solutions have been proposed for the management of construction debris, for telling stories of lost heritage for future generations and many other important problems, and these solutions bring hope. Many of the achievers discover their calling through their achievements at Ethos events.

Shantanu Subramaniam, for instance went on to pursue his postgraduation in Ancient Indian History and Archaeology after working on a project documenting the heritage of Hampi and is now an expert in architectural conservation.

While there have been many efforts that have come to light through our engagements, the reality of how many of these ideas see the light of day is rather dismal. We, as individuals and as a community of designers, have not been visible enough. It is now time for us designers to wake up, come together and be seen working with communities at different levels—be it in villages, towns or cities.

Design and architecture careers are largely seen as elitist professions that mostly city dwellers opt for. If students from small towns and villages are trained in architecture and design, we could have a community that is well-informed about ground realities and can respond appropriately to local needs and aspirations.

All these reflections led me to the intent of my walk, architects for a cause and the cause of architects as well.

---

[7]Risbud, Aniket. 'Urban Nomads—Housing for On-site Migrant Construction Workers at Thane', *ArchitectureLive!*, 26 December 2018, https://architecture.live/urban-nomads-housing-for-migrant-construction-workers-thane-aniket-risbud/#. Accessed on 22 November 2023.
[8]Sambyal, Swati Singh, Adishree Panda, Rinky Haldar and Ankit Gupta, 'SDG 11 and the Transition to Sustainable, Inclusive, and Resilient Cities', *Shelter*, Vol. 23, No. 2, 2022, 3–16.

CHAPTER 6

INDIA@75: THROUGH THE 1700/70 LENS

I wonder what this route would have looked like in 1947 when India gained independence. Conversations with people revealed that change was happening even as we spoke. Seventy-five, fifty, twenty-five or even five years ago, the road I walked on would have told different stories. Our population was around a mere 340 million seventy-five years ago,[9] it was close to 1.4 billion as I walked the 1700. Evidently, the number of people one came across on the roads and the density of the built environment would have been vastly different in 1947.

I can hardly imagine a time when a vehicle on the road made people run to gawk at it; a time when evenings and nights plunged whole villages into darkness; a time when natural water sources like wells, rivers and lakes were the primary source of water and agriculture was the primary occupation; a time when the postman held a place of great importance because he brought and read letters, delivered money orders, pensions and was the bearer of good and bad news; and a time when newspapers reached some of these locations a day or more later, as did the news.

It is indeed hard to imagine it because we seem to have come a long way since then. Highways and expressways cut through these villages and are the arteries and veins of our country that make it possible for people and goods to reach everywhere. Many of the roads I travelled through were of international standards and guidelines. Cars, trucks and lorries whizzed past me happily, their travel time considerably reduced. But this had me wondering—is 'international' exactly what we need? How would Chandni, the young lady I met in

---

[9]Schwartzberg, Joseph E., 'Demographic Trends—India', *Britannica*, https://www. britannica.com/place/India/Demographic-trends. Accessed on 23 November 2023.

Umari, Madhya Pradesh, get to her college across the highway? How would Rammohan steer his cattle safely along the expressway? How would Shakeel cycle in the midst of highway traffic from Churhat, his village, to reach the fields he worked in the neighbouring village of Gurh? Where would truck drivers, who are our lifeline in many ways, rest, eat and clean themselves with dignity? Our reality is different from that of other countries and the design of our roadways and ancillary infrastructure needs to reflect and cater to it.

When we were building the narrative around the walk, we discussed postmen as repositories of information about people and about how our country has changed. I was excited by the idea and decided that I would shadow a postman or postwoman at least in one location. While working on the route, I realized I would be passing Raibaghini post office in West Bengal. The name was evocative to me. We designed a presentation on stamps and Indian architecture to engage with those working at the Raibaghini post office. It was anticlimactic; this post office turned out to be a small, unimpressive building and was closed when I crossed it. This was indeed an eye-opener. Mobile phones, apps and electronic money transfers have replaced the old ways, even in remote locations, particularly after COVID. The postman had fallen from his pedestal. I also chose to mail postcards designed by our team to myself and friends from every location I stayed in. The most precious of these cards are the ones drawn on by schoolchildren during my interactions. Sadly, many friends have not yet received the postcards and I continued to receive a few stray ones even four months after I had completed the walk!

The ways of news and media have undergone huge changes. News travels in many new and different ways now. Newspapers are already a thing of the past for some people. I was impressed to find that internet connectivity was rather good throughout the journey, making communication and information dissemination much easier. As I was dressed for walking—in tights, a tee, shoes and a bandanna—and had a branded car following me, I attracted a lot of attention. I was stopped the first time by an ordinary-looking man, claiming to be from the press, a *patrakar*. I was quite taken aback. This reporter from Silli in Jharkhand overtook me on his scooter and stopped me with great excitement. He said he was returning from his morning errands when he saw me and hence, was not carrying his identification card. My team was a little hesitant when he wanted to shoot a video of me speaking about my intent to walk. I was completely game; my whole purpose was to reach people and I did not want to lose any opportunity of getting my message across. He asked me a few questions and recorded my responses as a video on his phone. Initially, I assumed he would use the video to write his piece, but this video was instead sent out through a news application and WhatsApp media to reach the community that was subscribed to it.

As I moved on, people accosted me all along the way as they had watched my video and it made me a bit of a celebrity. I was asked for selfies and many started following me on social media to keep in touch with my journey. Internet connectivity, technology and smartphones have certainly made people more aware, but digital disparity has now become another inequity that needs to be addressed. Those who can access information because they can afford smart devices and connectivity end up becoming more powerful than those who cannot. This was starkly evident during the pandemic.

Our country has come a long way since monarchy was abolished in 1950, but we still find the offspring of kings being revered. I observed common people sitting under trees, immediately standing and bowing when cars with families of the erstwhile rajas passed by. I met members of some of these royal families of the past and found them to be simple-hearted with a lot of goodwill to serve and make a difference. They displayed a desire to connect with the people of their region and address their problems, to improve infrastructure and to keep up with the times. We have all heard of bad pennies among them, but I was fortunate to have come across the good ones.

The last seventy-five years have seen the gaps between villages and towns reduced to the point of one almost overlapping with the other. There is hardly a visible difference now between villages and towns. Almost every village household has a family member working in the city to improve their lifestyle, and they bring in an urban influx of ideas and ways of doing things. My mind wandered to the number of rural folk who visit Kolkata to actually see the zoo and walk the maidan in winter and the number of people who participate in political rallies throughout the year in all the Indian cities. Such a simple visit to any city can change one's aspirations. Villagers who earlier led contented lives, who shared, cared and lived as one large family, have gradually changed as family members have migrated to cities and towns. Their acquisitions in the city and their ability or inability to better their lives have created chasms that are only growing deeper.

It appeared that those who migrate to cities and towns in search of prosperity experience privation. They move from airy and low-density environs to sharing a single room with many, from clean air to polluted surroundings, from simplicity of needs to a life made complex with aspirations that are often unattainable, from a sustainable lifestyle to the trappings of unsustainable urban habits. Helena Norberg-Hodge's book, *Ancient Futures: Learning from Ladakh*[10] resonates here with tales where city-based ills and malaise are often brought back as baggage to villages, disturbing the ecological balance and changing the paradigm.

I noticed the transition on all fronts as I moved across state borders. Speaking of state borders, a common pattern I observed was that the border villages and towns were the most neglected. The border regions had poorly developed roads (often just mudflat roads) and bad infrastructure. I surmised that by the time the government's plans could reach these border areas, the electoral term was probably near its end and there was no time to execute welfare schemes and infrastructural development. If a government could work the other way, from the outside to the inside, and choose to begin with these border regions immediately after it assumed its office, these towns and villages would not appear to be a no person's land.

While visible changes are there for all to see, the intangible must be inferred by observing how people interact and greet each other, how clusters of homes are formed, what people eat and how they live.

When I saw an old man touch a younger man's feet, questions raced through my mind: was he more learned, more affluent or was

---

[10]Norberg-Hodge, Helena, *Ancient Futures: Learning From Ladakh*, Sierra Club Books, Oakland, CA, 1991.

it an expression of caste supremacy? Similarly, the distance of a well—which is central to the lives of the villagers—from the village homes could be an indicator of who is allowed to use the well. When I was led by Rekha, an outspoken woman, to visit her house and I saw a smaller isolated outhouse with the woman's sister-in-law living in it, I asked myself, 'Had she been abandoned by her husband or vice versa? Was she a widow? Was she a rebel?' Through our conversation, I gathered that the unfortunate woman had lost her husband a couple of years ago and was thus living separately and frugally—much as a widow was expected to. Casual chats with people throughout the walk shed light on another truth about migration. While people moved to cities craving a better life, the definition of a better life also meant freedom from the shackles of caste, bonded labour, the ignominy of widowhood and other such oppressions. *My Father Baliah* by Y.B. Satyanarayana,[11] a book I read a couple of years ago, tells such a story of migration that saved a family from the evils of caste.

I encountered wise people who would have been but children or young adults in 1947. I saw monuments and simple homes that had weathered time's vagaries. My gaze often travelled between the wrinkles on people's faces and the signs of weathering I saw on old buildings, evoking a sense of nostalgia and a yearning to know more.

---

[11]Satyanarayana, Y.B., *My Father Baliah*, HarperCollins, Gurugram, 21 December 2011.

CHAPTER 7

THE 1700/70 ROUTE AND MORE

112 Days Before the Flag-off
22 October 2021

'The path from dreams to success does exist. May you have the vision to find it, the courage to get on to it, and the perseverance to follow it.'

—KALPANA CHAWLA

Those who know me know my proclivity to plan in great detail. I am restless and have sleepless nights if there is a task left with loose ends. And hence, I first began to meticulously plan the route. For the campaign to have maximum impact, I felt that the route needed to end at the national capital, New Delhi. Kolkata, being my place of residence for two decades and my place of birth, was the perfect choice as the starting point.

The shortest route from Kolkata to Delhi was 1,417 km with a large portion cutting through Uttar Pradesh. I mapped out the route, including all the stopovers with possible accommodations, and voila! I thought I had the perfect route! I had even ensured that Varanasi, Amethi, Ayodhya and Lucknow—places I was excited about exploring—were a part of my journey. I knew that the elections in Uttar Pradesh and Punjab were due to take place, but I was not aware of the dates. I was warned by a friend to look up the dates and when I did, February 2022 to March 2022 stared back at me. Walking through a state that was in the throes of elections was not exactly what I had had in mind for my walking experience.

Back to scratch. I started reworking the route—this time taking a detour via Madhya Pradesh for the most part once I crossed Jharkhand. Uttar Pradesh's expanse would have to wait for another day, hopefully not for long. This change added around 250 km to my journey, but that did not deter me. I was excited about adding another state to my itinerary. I would be walking through West Bengal, Jharkhand, Uttar Pradesh, Madhya Pradesh, Rajasthan, Haryana and Delhi—a total of around 1,700 km if the walking off-route to different places for interactions was included!

I initially overestimated my endurance and planned to walk over 35 km on most days, and even over 40 km on some days. As I had commenced my training by then, it gradually dawned on me that I needed to set realistic expectations of myself. Not only did I have to meet these long-distance goals day after day for the duration of the trip, but I had also planned a high-intensity trip. Such journeys usually begin with short targets and gently ramp up. Most importantly, this was not a test of my physical endurance but an adventure, a journey of discovery. I needed energy every day to meet, interact, empathize, smile and laugh. I revisited my route map often and recalibrated the numbers until I had a difficult but attainable goal at hand.

1,700 km in 60–75 days!

I then went on to research others who had attempted such feats around the world, and those who had done so specifically in India. I read with wonder the story of Nipun Mehta shared by Mahesh Daas, a friend and the President of the Boston Architectural College—a partner to my initiative. Nipun Mehta and his wife, Guri, chose to give up their lucrative jobs in the US, sold all their belongings and reached India; they started walking from Gandhi Ashram towards the south of India. They walked 1,000 km over three months and subsisted on the generosity of strangers. Their walk was a quest for higher truth. The kind of mental strength and surrender required for a walk of this nature is of a different order. I came across Siddharth Agarwal who, in 2016–17, followed the river Ganga from Gangasagar in West Bengal to its source in the Himalayas[12]—a 3,000 km walk that took 10

---

[12]Majumdar, Meghna, 'The Man Who Follows India's Rivers on Foot', *The Hindu*, 21 February 2021, https://www.thehindu.com/sci-tech/energy-and-environment/the-man-who-follows-indias-rivers-on-foot/article33893634.ece. Accessed on 23 November 2023.

months to complete. Herman Hesse has said in his all-time great novel, *Siddhartha,* 'The river is everywhere...'[13] I am sure that Siddharth Agarwal's walk helps him feel the river's presence even today, wherever he is. Closer to home, I was introduced to Srishti Bakshi, who used to be a colleague of my husband, Bala. She launched her organization, Women of My Billion (WOMB), after she walked around 3,500 km from Kanyakumari to Kashmir, which took her around eight months. I managed to connect with Srishti, which turned out to be quite the turning point. Chatting with someone who had been there and done it was reassuring. My relationship with Srishti deepened over a period of time and through the duration of my walk too. Such missions make you see life from a different lens and make you large-hearted. Srishti generously shared about her trip, pointed out things to me that I had not considered, kept in touch through the planning stages and offered ample advice. She introduced me to Vinayak, who had been a part of her team, and he came on board as my on-ground team manager.

After our first virtual meeting with Vinayak, my family heaved a sigh of relief. We had always been sure that there would be a car accompanying me with my things, but we now knew that Vinayak, who would be driving the vehicle, would be responsible for shadowing me closely to ensure my safety, would assist with the navigation, would manage logistics for planned and spontaneous events and interactions and would locate and coordinate on accommodation—all according to the plan! We recruited Dhanraj to support Vinayak. Parameshwar, a videographer and the director for the moving content, and Shantanu, a photographer, formed the documentation team. The back-end team at Ethos managed the content for interactions, checklist for documentation and social media and took on the work of identifying communities and organizations for interactive sessions.

We made a detailed list of all the gear we would need for my physical fitness, nutrition and documentation, and began ticking off the checklist. I read up on different types of shoes, what to invest in and bought two new pairs of shoes and broke into them a month ahead of the trip.

---

[13]Hesse, Herman. *Siddhartha,* Buccaneer Books, Cutchogue, NY, 1976.

Two months before the trip, I decided that it was time to connect with my well-wishers and tap into relationships that had blossomed over the years. I wrote to friends from school, architects and sponsors who had aligned with us through our events in the past and requested their support. And boy, did I get support! As it is often said, when there is a powerful idea, the universe comes together to ensure its realization.[14]

I connected with a fitness expert, TimTim Sharma, to get some tips on endurance training. TimTim patiently spent a lot of time with me and told me that I may not benefit from having a regular coach on such a journey; I was already listening to my body and keeping up with my training and hence, I was my best coach. She offered her shoulder whenever the pain would become difficult to bear. She did not use the word 'if', but the word 'when' because we already knew that there would be pain. I spoke to a nutritionist, Vaishali Ratnam, who was kind enough to draw out a nutrition plan that began a month before I set off. I met with a sports and rehabilitation doctor, Dr Sanjay Chatterjee, who was really excited about the adventure I was embarking on. I also informed our general physician, Dr Sandeep Sangar, to expect my SOS. As the virus had caught up with me, I got a complete blood picture done. I even got dental work done (as prescribed by the dentist) before I set off so that a toothache would be the last thing I would need to worry about.

---

[14]All the people who have played a major role in nurturing this idea to fruition have been credited in the *Gratitude Wall* at the end of the book.

CHAPTER 8

FROM A WOMAN IN A HURRY
TO A WOMAN IN NO HURRY

91 Days Before the Flag-off
13 November 2021

Practice and training gave me the confidence I needed. Pain was a nourishment to my courage.

I took to running in 2014, at the age of forty-five. I put in my name for the Tata Steel Kolkata 10K (TSK 10K) run and registered my husband and sons as well. I then went to town with the news that I was running my first 10K on 28 December. Because the world knew, there was no turning back. Bala and I started training for it and completed the run within a reasonable time. But it took me a couple of years to be able to run 10 km at a stretch. In my second 10K run the following year, I was pleasantly surprised to find myself in the third position in my age category. I edged my way to the first position in my third effort. This gave me the impetus to advance to a half marathon. We got a professional coach to ensure that we were doing things right. I completed the TSK 25K in 2017 and achieved podium finishes in my age category in the subsequent 21 km runs organized by the Kolkata Police. I now found myself contemplating the extreme—running a full marathon. 42.195 km is indeed a long distance and I needed to have a different level of mental and physical fitness to achieve that feat. It is essential to mention here that fitness through running and walking are not my profession and I need to eke out time to train outside of my work hours that are quite demanding.

My coach, Dharmendra,—'D' as he is called by his trainees—set weekly routines that were interesting challenges and they kept me invested in my training. Of course, there were moments of despair and that was when I called a friend—actually many different friends depending on the kind of encouragement I needed. I understood the importance of nutrition and recovery. I am a vegetarian, so I had to revisit my diet to include a lot of protein. I took to running wherever I was. I ran when we were on vacations in Moscow, Saint Petersburg, Haifa in Israel, Galle in Sri Lanka, Norway, Boston, Pittsburgh, Alaska and on the deck of a cruise ship! I ran in almost every city, town and village I visited in India. I took part in the TCS Amsterdam Half Marathon and was nowhere near my personal best in it. My father was on his deathbed at the time and this made me perceive the power of one's state of mind. I lost my father soon after the Amsterdam run.

I persisted with my training through these peaks and troughs to run my first 42.195 km in 2019 with a great sense of achievement. I kept running during the pandemic, even if it was only around a small restricted circuit, and completed my third full marathon virtually. Running during difficult times has helped me retain my sanity and keep calm. Thinking back, our lives would have been bereft without the magic of running.

Almost through the pandemic in 2021, I was running 21 km every weekend, not to mention the gentler 8–12 km twice during the week. I would walk for two days every week and follow it up with exercises to build lower body strength. When training for a race, the routine consisted of three running days a week. This included an interval run, which involved alternating sprints of different distances with jogging; the tempo run, which alternated between running at a steady pace for specified durations and jogging; and the heart rate long run on weekends, where the goal was to maintain a safe heart rate while covering long distances. I still struggle with maintaining a low heart rate. The long training runs progressed from one hour to four hours for a full marathon. Every run would be preceded by gentle warm-up exercises and stretches and would end with a cooling jog, followed by stretches.

Despite my intense activities, it would be wrong to assume that I was without any health problems. In fact, a doctor once called me a rag doll after seeing all the scars from sutures on my abdomen. I had my first surgery when I was twenty-two, followed by extensive treatment for endometriosis. Thankfully, despite the endometriosis, I had two normal conceptions and deliveries. I also had to undergo two more surgeries and a couple of laparoscopic procedures. Probably as a result of one such hospitalization, I was afflicted with tuberculosis when I was around twenty-nine, which took its own course. When I touched forty, I began suffering from pain in the small joints like my knuckles and was diagnosed with rheumatoid arthritis. I was then advised by a cousin, also a doctor, to make exercise a religion, and that is what I did. I took to working out in the gym until the advertisement for the 10K run caught my eye and the running bug bit me.

But now that I was taking on this mammoth task, I had to teach myself to walk. When it comes to long distances, walking is a lot tougher, at least for me. It meant that I would have to stay on my feet for so much longer. I had signed up for another full marathon three months before I was scheduled to begin my walk, but I was advised against it by experts. Therefore, I stuck to walking. I began with an hour and moved on to five to six hours in total, with a short break in between for a sandwich. I walked the banks of the river, the different bridges of the city, went to homes of idol-makers in Kumartuli, had my sandwich sitting on the ghats, walked through old Kolkata, walked to Ramakrishna Mission in Narendrapur, walked in the rain, walked before daybreak, walked in the sun—yes, I walked and walked. There was one occasion when Bala was taking a flight to Chennai. I went with him to the airport and walked the 25-kilometre distance back. Training and walking such long distances were hard, but this journey was not going to be easy and I had to get used to the pain. I carried a small backpack and loaded it with packets of rice, dal, sugar and whatever was available, to get used to carrying some weight as well. I had once taken a kilogram of peanuts with me; Bala had spent the whole morning looking for peanuts at home for a dish that was being prepared, little knowing that it was carefully stowed in my backpack a few kilometres away!

As I combed the streets of Kolkata with great joy, I tried to see this city from the memories of my parents and tried to imagine its future too. I discovered nooks, corners and facets of this beautiful city and realized that every city has many hearts, and they all need to throb in unison to keep it going.

✑

73 Days Before the Flag-off
2 December 2021

When the first poster was launched for the #WalkForArcause campaign, the reactions to the announcement evoked a multitude of emotions in me, especially gratitude, because I had such a wonderful universe of friends and well-wishers who were not only encouraging me but also offering all kinds of help and support. I suddenly felt butterflies in my stomach as my dream was taking shape and becoming real. There were people who offered to drive the car for me, to drive along and look out for me, who contributed generously, who connected us with people who could help in case of an emergency along the way, who arranged for accommodation at different places—in company guest houses, government circuit houses, college hostels, hotels—and more. Herman, the sceptical friend I had mentioned earlier, put his full might behind me and made so many impossible things possible.

This was not a time when I could afford to shy away from accepting help. I, unabashedly, latched on to all the support I could get. I had to decline offers of people accompanying me for long stretches along the route because this was completely new terrain for me. I was not sure what hurdles I would encounter and could only afford to manage myself on this challenge. Secondly, I had also realized that this needed to be a solitary journey on many levels, to lead me inwards and onwards.

I was also bombarded with incredulous reactions and questions. Had I reached beyond my limits this time? Would my body take it? Was it safe? There were practical and sensible questions like: How would I keep myself nourished along the way? How would I find toilets on the route? I felt queasy.

Doubts began gnawing at my resolve.

But I sat back, closed my eyes and reflected on the magic of the idea! I marvelled at the beauty and the power of what I was embarking on.

I would have the opportunity to connect with so many people, to listen to their tales and get a glimpse into their lives and their problems. I may have the good fortune of playing Holi with one of the communities and be washed by the pre-Holi showers of Madhya Pradesh. I could see my hobby and my profession coming together in complete harmony. I would watch them breathe meaning and vivacity into each other.

One question was thrown at me by multiple people. Why was I walking and not cycling or taking a vehicle from point to point? I needed to address this. Not just for those who were curious, but for myself as well. This adventure was neither intended as a path-breaking one nor as a path-making one. I looked at this as a path-finding mission. When we are on a search, whether it is for something one has lost or in search of a destination or a master, we need to slow down. The slower the pace the better, so that we do not miss signs and directions that are out there.

Plus, walking is a great leveller; boundaries and disparities seem to blur while walking because most people can work at matching paces. A smile here, a wave there, a nod and a word and you have struck up a connection, maybe even a conversation.

Creating a sense of ease, fostering familiarity and encouraging people to share with, care for and open up to one another was the intent of this pilgrimage. And a pilgrimage it was! The bonds, interactions and overall experience served as the deity, temple and prayer, all rolled into one.

That was when I decided to make sure to take my senses with me every time I walked on this journey.

CHAPTER 9

WHILE MY CITY GENTLY SLEEPS

Being one with silence as the sky moves from darkness to light is powerful.

Watching the first rays of the sun gently washing over the fields, ponds, treetops and buildings makes for a perfect start to a day. I watched people paying obeisance to the sun as the city stirred to life. I heard the clangs of pots and pans as roadside eateries serving chai-nashta (tea and breakfast) got ready for their customers. The smells of masalas being fried for the traditional luchi-aloo (puri and potato curry) wafted into my nostrils as I walked.

I admired the nifty innovations people devise for storing their possessions, securing their property at night and making the most of the meagre space they have. These low-cost or no-cost interventions include a simple plank of plywood cantilevered under a railing to act as a seat on one side and a low table for storage on the other side, and a Canna leaf placed under a broken pipe to ensure that the water is let out where it should. I was inspired! I marvelled at what common sense and a little thought to design could do. While these were attempts at jugaad design and DIY solutions, they brought my attention back to the power of design in bettering the lives of people at large.

As I walked through the streets, I felt like I was in a time warp. Graceful buildings from over a century ago were juxtaposed horizontally and sometimes vertically, with swanky modern buildings. Gnarled roots and trees were growing out of structures, which were so dilapidated that a gentle nudge might have brought them crashing down. Mansions with large gardens were next to hovels on the road. The level of the road, sometimes higher than the floor level of the adjoining homes, reminded me that I was walking on layers of history.

Italo Calvino describes many fictitious cities in his book, *Invisible Cities*.[15] Cities over cities, cities within cities, cities in your mind, a city that stays awake, silent cities, cities for those not living, cities with no garbage, cities of garbage, cities with no air or sky, ethereal cities. I saw them all around me in this one city of mine. I wondered how many more cities would be amalgamated into this city over time.

Most of our cities began organically and may not have been planned. These are usually the older parts of our cities, which throb with character even today, despite the chaos that reigns in them. The planned cities are developed around these old cities, and it is in the burgeoning outer layers that one can sometimes come across evidence of a lack of understanding of urban design, a lack of empathy in design and even greed. Empathy in design is essential to understand the user's perspective as well as the context and it is central for the development of sensitive and compassionate design solutions that nurture a sense of belonging.

As I meandered through different parts of the city, the transformation of people from those who exude warmth and sensitivity to those who are too preoccupied with their own lives hit me. I felt a chill running down my spine as this realization dawned.

Is design responsible? Is design in fact that powerful?

---

[15]Calvino, Italo, *Invisible Cities*, Random House, Manhattan, NY, 2010.

Walk,
to explore.
Walk,
to discover.
Walk,
inwards.
Walk,
outwards.
Walk,
and you shall arrive.

CHAPTER 10

FLAG-OFF

Day 1
13 February 2022

'A journey of a thousand miles begins with a single step.'

—LAO TZU

Lao Tzu seems to have had me in mind when he wrote this. I began a journey that was a little over 1,000 miles with the first step beginning from Victoria Memorial in Kolkata.

When I sit to recall the night before I set off, I draw an absolute blank. I do not remember what I ate for my last meal before I left home. It is all a blur. The week before D-day was spent ensuring that we had all the things I needed to carry because we would mostly be at a distance from large cities. Ordering online and coordinating deliveries on the move would not be easy. On the previous day, Shubhayan Modak, a young architect, had organized an urban storytelling, walking tour through quintessential Kolkata, titled 'People Places Perspectives'.

We were to flag off at 8 a.m. and a small crowd of almost sixty people had gathered around 7.30 a.m. to see me off, while many joined in virtually. This included friends, morning walkers and joggers, students, architects, representatives from organizations that had extended their support to this initiative, neighbours and housekeeping staff. All of them had come with a heart full of good wishes that carried me through the trip. The event was short and sweet, with people speaking about their expectations and expressing their surprise and admiration for the initiative. There were more waves than hugs, thanks to the pandemic rearing its head again. Omicron had also ensured that this crowd would be small. And before I knew it, it was 8 a.m.

Showstopper 2

In keeping with the spirit of the walk, I decided that two construction workers, Prashanta Naskar and Vijay Sharma, would flag me off, along with five students studying architecture at local colleges in Kolkata— Jadavpur University; Indian Institute of Engineering Science and Technology, Shibpur; Amity School of Architecture and Planning; and Techno India University. Prashanta and Vijay had been pursuing this craft for close to thirty years and had learnt it from their fathers. Both had children who had chosen to educate themselves in the hope of taking on alternate professions, having witnessed the hardships that their fathers had to undergo. To me, construction workers are the spine of the industry and students are the future; it was important for both of them to be with me as I started this journey to highlight important issues relevant to the construction and design community. It wasn't easy to identify two construction workers, which is a story on its own and I will dwell on it later. I also tried to bring a female construction worker to walk the first few steps with me, but the number of women on site in Kolkata had dwindled to none during the pandemic.

I began by honouring Prashanta and Vijay and expressed my gratitude to the construction workers of India.

Dot on schedule, we had Prashanta, Vijay and the young minds wave the flags and the banners, and off I went. I walked from Victoria Memorial onto Red Road, past Eden Gardens, through Strand Road and onto Howrah Bridge. There were many who had told me that they would walk at least the first 10 km with me. But only four friends—Hermanprit Singh, the police officer; Binwant, a professor at NIFT, Kolkata; Pritha Basu and Rashni Parichha, both architects— accompanied me till the end of Howrah Bridge, a distance of around 8 km. After this, Bala and I made our way to Dankuni, which marked the end of Day 1 at 26 km.

Thus began the adventure of a lifetime!

I was stepping out of my comfort zone into a vast unknown. No amount of training or preparation can get you ready for this experience. You do not know what challenges will befall you and when. You have to think on your feet to meet these challenges—literally and metaphorically! I was only going to discover the same as I stepped forward.

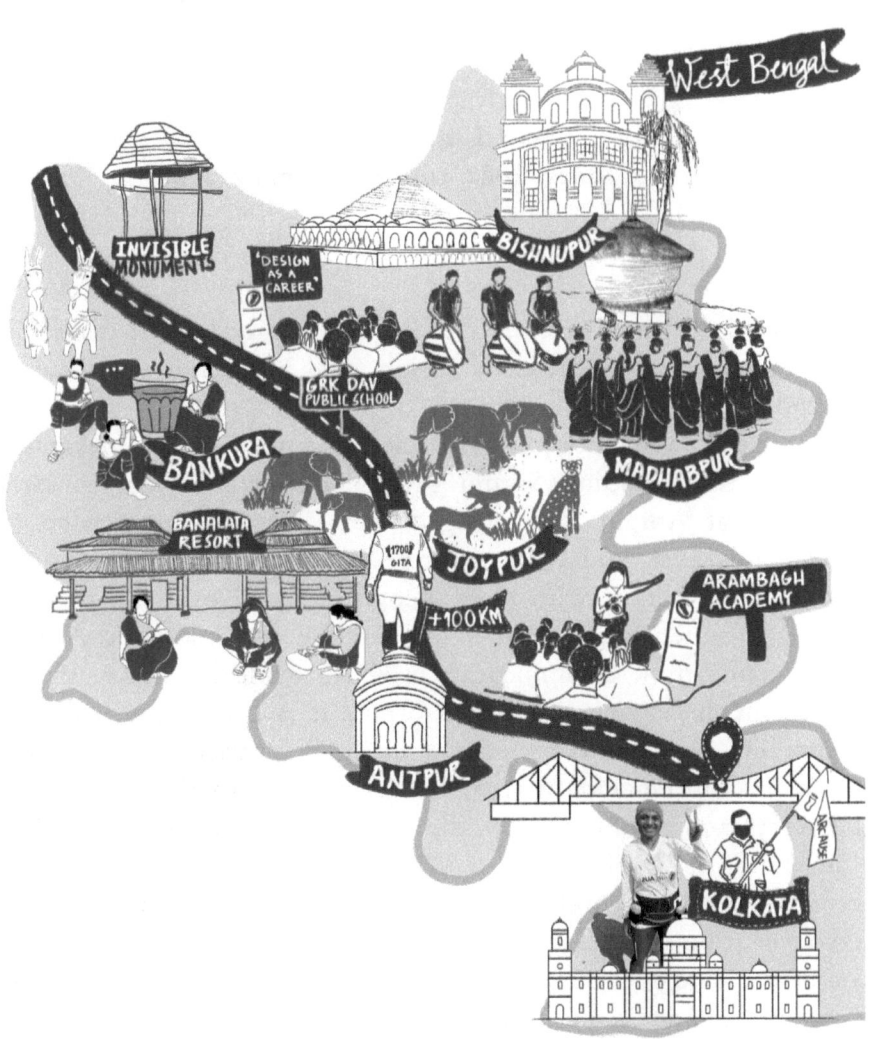

CHAPTER 11

BENGAL SETS THE PACE AND MOOD

Day 1 to Day 13
13 February 2022 to 25 February 2022

Showstopper 3

I had heard of Antpur from a friend, and he insisted that I make this place a stop on my walk. Only 55 km from Kolkata, it was close to my end point on Day 2.

On 24 December 1886, nine disciples of Ramakrishna Paramahamsa, including Swami Vivekananda, are known to have assembled at Antpur and pledged their lives to the service of humankind. Even today the anniversary of this historic event is celebrated in Antpur with many people from all over the country coming together. Legend has it that Antpur, also known as Aatpur, got its name from a zamindar, Atar Khan, while others say that it came from the eight villages that formed it. A part of the Jangipara community development block of Hooghly district, Antpur boasts of the Radha Govind Jiu temple, a terracotta wonder built after the temples of Bishnupur in the eighteenth century by Krishna Ram Mitra of Bardhaman Raj. With this temple, the splendour of terracotta moved beyond Bishnupur. The intent was to capture Hindu fervour during a time of invasions by Muslim kings and European companies. The guide, Sudip Mitra, proudly told me that while the Bishnupur temples were older, this temple was taller at 100 feet. He also waxed eloquent about the thatched wooden chandimandap (the altar for a village goddess) and showed the intricate wooden carvings on the pillars and beams. This was the first time that I had seen a thatched temple on such a grand scale.

As I concluded my third day at Kotulpur, I was offered the premises of the traffic police control room for my exercises. Amusingly, I saw the locals peeping in, walking in purposefully and marching out immediately—just to catch a glimpse of me. When I emerged, there were close to a hundred people waiting to know what I was doing in their vicinity. That is when I realized that it was working! The potential of reaching out to people and learning from them—the magic had already begun to unfold. After chatting with them, I set out again with a spring in my step.

My first interaction at Arambagh Vivekananda Academy merits special mention. The principal, Sudhamoy Mondal, had received the National Award for Teachers (instituted in 1958) from the President of India and was an inspiring and humble personality. I addressed the students of Class 10, all of whom pleasantly surprised me with their awareness and sharpness on all topics—art, science, career choices, etc. What further impressed me was their confidence. The students were not shy while asking questions or responding to mine. This was a trait that I noticed in most schools that I visited.

Showstopper 4

On our way to Bankura the day before, we had stopped at Banalata at the suggestion of a local policeman to savour posto vadas (poppy-seed fritters), a local delicacy. Banalata is a tourist resort largely managed by the women of the surrounding villages and a beautiful interaction with the workers ensued.

Anjali, to me, was the showstopper of the day.

Anjali lives in Joypur with her family and works at the resort. With her guileless smile, she openly shared details about their lives. This interaction was the beginning of many more, and it showcased to me the joy found in simple living. Anjali articulated to me the benefits of her simple mud home, but coyly divulged that she is saving up for a brick-and-mortar home; this preference had developed as it was a trend. This led to a prolonged discussion about homes with Anjali and her friends, Parvati and Mondira, by the end of which they were open to bucking the trend after assessing and exploring the pros and cons of choosing a certain way of building their homes. Despite my differences from them, a kinship developed and it surfaced again when I visited them six months later on my way to Bishnupur to meet the local MLA. They did not take a second to recognize me, even though I was wearing a saree this time around, and we chatted as if we were long-lost friends. They served me a hearty meal that I ate in the company of my driver.

Showstopper 5

Our first rest day involved less rest and more action, and I had no regrets about it at all. An interaction had been arranged with the Adivasi community at Madhabpur, a nearby village. We reached according to schedule but realized that the community needed more time to organize themselves. We gave them space to get ready and I used that hour to clock some miles because the route was not too far away. When we returned, the place had been transformed!

All the inhabitants of Madhabpur had gathered and were dressed for the occasion. The women wore traditional white sarees with red borders and floral jewellery. I was welcomed by the sounds of drums played by men, while the women danced to the beat. There were old women, young women, little girls and a boy dancing too. I was garlanded, and to my initial horror, gently drawn into the ring of dancers. I say horror because I do not use the expression 'I have two left feet' lightly. I seem to freeze when I am expected to sway to music. And here I was! In the company of simple souls who had welcomed me into their world, I so longed to make their stories mine and be a part of theirs. I suddenly found myself completely at ease and moving elegantly, even if I say so myself. I moved away after a while, and they continued to dance in a circle around me while some customary rituals—getting me to wash my feet with water and application of a mixture of vermillion and rice to my forehead—were being performed by members of the community. This interaction was facilitated by a Bishnupur-based NGO, Mallabhum Prayas.

We spent the next hour in an unfinished building talking about their lives and their homes. The latter was really the reason I was there—to understand how they lived and how they wished to live. I showed them a presentation titled 'Amar Badi' or 'Mera Ghar', which means 'my home', with the intention of learning from them as well as arousing their curiosity to gain more information when they choose to build afresh or upgrade their homes. They had many questions and were also perplexed to learn about the different layers that go into creating a home.

Surbala was one of the most vocal among the gathered women. Her daughter, Malati, was studying to be the first female graduate of the village. The community was often hired for events—political and otherwise—to sing and dance. The men complained about not having enough money to buy themselves the drums that were belting out the beats. I shrank at the thought that they had actually rented the drums for me! I was told that the cost of a set of drums was ₹25,000, and when I asked if they had a bank account for the troupe they sadly responded in the negative.

We discussed the benefits of organizing themselves if they wished to use their performances to earn a living. Most of their earnings came from farming, which I soon realized was a pattern as I went along. Potatoes were a major crop in the region. They also grew groundnuts and leafy vegetables in rotation.

Surbala led me to her home and I was delighted to see the warm mud-dwelling. We saw a snake winding its way around her kitchen, adjacent to the main home. While a couple from my team jumped, the family was unperturbed and seemed perfectly comfortable with the reptile in their habitat, like we city-bred folks would be with a cat or a dog for a pet. Across the street from Surbala's home was a half-complete dwelling recently built with modern materials; it seemed incongruous in its surroundings. A peek inside revealed that this home was warmer, darker and less ventilated, and we chatted about these differences.

A fitting finale to my visit to Madhabpur was a delightful, humble meal of puffed rice and dried pea curry—muri and ghughni, as it is known, with fresh green chillies, lemon and cucumber. The whole village sat in a circle around a boiling pot of pea curry, with me as their guest. I was given the honour of being seated first. We ate from donas (or leaf plates). I thought to myself, 'What indeed do I have to give? I only have so much to receive!'

Months after this visit, I returned to the community, this time with an apt gift—a set of drums so that they would not have to borrow or rent them again. I was happy to be a part of the inauguration of a concept for a school to be headed by Malati. Little Akash and Sonali signed their names on the whiteboard and dreamed of becoming a doctor and a schoolteacher, respectively. I hope they are able to chase their dreams and the world makes their path exciting and their destination attainable.

Showstopper 6

Bishnupur, the erstwhile capital of the Hindu Mallabhum kingdom, surely would have been resplendent in its heyday with its terracotta treasures, each built between the sixteenth and the eighteenth centuries. Does it evoke any of that awe today? While the individual temples, such as the Pancha Ratna temple and the Madangopal temple, to name a couple, are still a joy that hold one's gaze, the town certainly needs a lot more attention. A walk through the city at night and again during the day highlighted to me the need for an integrated approach while conserving our heritage. If the focus is only on individual structures and art and does not address people, livelihoods, economy and more, restoration becomes rather unsustainable.

Showstopper 7

The same is true for crafts. Bhairavnath Pal is unique to Parbatipur, which is where he continues his occupation. He is the only remaining idol maker there and has kept his passion alive!

He learnt the trade and skill from his father, whom he used to assist throughout his childhood and well into his youth. He lovingly kneads the clay, claiming to be as good at making idols out of cement. He is also an artist who paints gods and goddesses, he says. Festivals such as Saraswati Puja, Durga Puja and Kali Puja are busy periods when people order idols. He is a one-man army and handles all the tasks from purchasing the raw materials and making the idols ready for despatch to soliciting business and negotiating deals. He has a son who has completed B.Ed but is currently without a job. The son prefers sitting idle to joining his father in the family business, he says. But Bhairavnath forges ahead, despite knowing fully well that there is no one in the entire village to whom he can hand over the baton.

Beginner's Woes

My resilience was tested straightaway on the second day of the walk. I had spent the last three weeks breaking into two new pairs of shoes. Unfortunately, I allowed the frugal side of me to override my better judgement and chose to wear an old, worn-out pair of shoes thinking I would discard them in a few days, little realizing the consequences. At the end of three hours, the Achilles tendon of my right foot began to hurt, and I struggled to walk. I still trudged along at a reasonable pace and covered 28 km. Bala had accompanied me until Day 2, but I was on my own from Day 3.

This injury led to a week-long struggle and I realized why the Achilles heel is often called a vulnerable spot. In the days that followed, the pain was a constant as I continued to meet my targets. The crew noticed my discomfort from my altered gait. I chose to walk and not run and began to worry—I was just off the starting block and could ill afford a setback so early. I connected with friends who were serious fitness enthusiasts to get their point of view. I consulted with a physiotherapist via video call and spoke to a doctor as well. Satish Gujaran, an ultra-runner, a comrade marathoner and a coach, who had been introduced to me by an architect and friend, Kiran Kapadia, was quite calm and reassuring. He comforted me by saying that I would slip into the groove in no time.

Sure enough, it hurt for a few days and then, I gradually added running to my daily routine. I learned a lot from different people during this 10-day period. While I was used to a routine for my runs, I realized that I needed to follow a very different regimen now. I began using the foam roller in the morning before I started from my room, accompanied by a few stretches; I completed a warm-up routine at my starting point. The stretches and the roller were repeated whenever I took a break and I ended with a longer routine of the same exercises.

The first rest day turned out to be quite an active one. It was after the second week of walking that I started to feel the need for rest—at least one day a week to actually help me rejuvenate. My second rest day at Jamshedpur turned out to be just that. I walked until Jhalda on the border of West Bengal. From there we drove to Jamshedpur, which was not on our walking route. We drove back to Jhalda a day later to resume my journey. We received an extremely warm welcome from the Jharkhand Chapter of the Indian Institute of Architects (IIA). The presentation by Amitava Ghosh, an activist who works with tribals, was quite an eye-opener on the lifestyles and struggles of the community. The stories he narrated made even more sense thanks to our visit to Madhabpur. Besides hosting an interaction and a dinner, Nalin Goel from IIA Jharkhand was kind enough to arrange for a session with the TATA High Performance Centre (HPC). After a tour around the centre by Mukul Choudhari, Sukdeb Mahanta spent a good half-a-day with me, teaching me stretches that would help me and prescribing a routine too. In addition, my limbs were pulled and muscles were kneaded, and I was also put on cryotherapy for my lower limbs. This was a much-needed pit stop.

Sukdeb grew to be another friend I could call upon when in trouble with my limbs, muscles and bones. As I left the centre, I hoped that all would go well so that I would need to call him only after the walk was over— to convey my gratitude.

Jamshedpur lived up to its reputation of being a well-laid-out industrial town. While we drove through large tree-lined avenues, we also saw sections that had developed organically and some areas that were not as sanitary as other parts of Jamshedpur. While the road from Jamshedpur to Jhalda was extremely smooth in sections, a large portion that was under repair made me wish that I was walking instead. The municipal elections in West Bengal were to be held the next day, and the whole route this far from Kolkata to Jhalda had a festive look. There were colourful festoons, loudspeakers and rallies. When we reached Jhalda late that evening, I decided to complete a couple of kilometres on my route before reaching our accommodation and it was exciting to walk while jostling through some crowded areas. We left early in the morning on the next day, and fortunately missed all the madness that makes an election day in India!

I bid goodbye to West Bengal as it stepped into the throes of the election frenzy on voting day.

CHAPTER 12

WALK WITH YOUR SENSES

A few years ago, I had taken my mother to get her fitted with a hearing aid. I was delighted when she joyfully exclaimed that she distinctly heard the distant tweeting of a bird. Suddenly, I was rudely jolted by the realization that I had failed to hear that chirp of the bird—not because I could not, but because I chose not to. I had allowed other preoccupations to mask this simple joy.

Oftentimes, I indulge in a simple exercise when I go out on a run or a walk. I spend a few minutes exclusively dedicated to each of my senses. In my time with my visual senses, I soak in all that I see and try not to miss any detail—the colours of the sarees drying on balconies, the patterns of the railings, the shapes of the clouds, the barks on the trees, the missing alphabet in a sentence—while taking in the whole visage too. Seeing with such focus leads to the development of enhanced skills of observing, assessing, inferring and understanding. For instance, I see a lever when a bag of cement is being tilted with a rod before a worker hoists it on his back, and I understand the principle of centre of gravity when I notice him adjusting the bag before walking. Or I look at the colours of nature and try and guess what colours come together to make it!

I did experiment with this technique quite a bit on this journey as well. I devised small games to help me tide through difficult days. Predicting exactly where I would complete 300 metres became a game that I grew to excel at. I would mark out a tree, a building or a sign that to me appeared 300 metres away. Initially, I was often off the mark, but I gradually got a perfect score almost every time.

I soon knew how many reflectors on the road or how many repetitive patterns on the railings made a kilometre!

My auditory senses had an important role to play in keeping me safe, and it was important for me to hone them. During my training,

I would spend a few minutes every day taking in every sound around me, distant and close. I paid attention to the sounds of vehicles—whether they were to my right, my left, behind me, or coming towards me. As the sun lit up the sky every day, I moved from silence and experienced the hum of life growing into a cacophony with the chirping of birds, mooing of cows, calls of prayer, people's chatter and honking on the roads. I enhanced my awareness of the sounds that elevated my spirit, those that bothered me and those that I was indifferent to. I usually avoid listening to music when I am walking or running because I prefer to engage with the sounds around me. However, during the 1700, there were certain parts of each day, and sometimes entire days, where I found that music was making me feel as if I was walking in the rain. The attention to the sense of sound seemed to aptly align with my mood. There were times when the song I was listening to answered a question that I had asked. Conversations between the unsaid and the lilting voices were uplifting. I found myself stepping to the beats of Shankar–Ehsaan–Loy and R.D. Burman, and my fingers tapped to the taalam or beats when T.M. Krishna and Aruna Sairam held a concert for me. 'Here Comes the Sun' and 'Sunshine on My Shoulders' brought solace over the first few days when the temperatures were pleasant, but the same numbers were ominous as I marched through 43°C.

I touched, felt and learnt from tree trunks, leaves, mud walls, bricks, plastic, plaster, thatch, wooden benches, bitumen, mud roads, concrete, rubber, grass, dried cow-dung cakes, fabric, people and plenty more.

Close your eyes and allow your tactile senses to take over. Understand the emotions that textures can evoke. Does the aesthetic of a mud wall with hand-painted designs on it appeal only because of the visual beauty or does the coarse rawness of it have a role in making it attractive?

The wind helped me deal with the heat, and I would quickly dab ice and water on my head and face to use it to my advantage. But walking against the wind also meant I had to make more of an effort. As I moved between the vastness of the rural to the denser urban areas every so often, I witnessed the heat island effect. I walked through challenges faced by many pedestrians, walking on roads that heavily favour vehicles with hardly any shoulder and with uneven surfaces. A steep camber on the roadside meant I was walking at an angle most of the time, resulting in one of my lower limbs and my hips always being under stress. Even in places where there was a pedestrian path, the surface material of the path was the same as that of the vehicular road, making it a hazard for the knees.

Exploring the sense of taste while walking is a challenge. For nutrition and energy, I had nuts, dates, dried figs, apricots, energy bars and gels hidden in the pouch around my waist. I usually had a peanut butter sandwich when I took my break, a banana when I started and a protein shake and tender coconut water as I closed my walk for the day. Having the same meals every single day for almost seventy days can quickly become torturous. I learnt to savour each bite as I imagined them nourishing and invigorating me. While I did focus on the literal sense of taste, I also explored the figurative 'taste'—as in the ability to discern what is of good quality and how it leads to our preferential tastes of colour, fabric, styles, lifestyles, food, habits, faith, profession and brands.

I found the olfactory sense (of smell) a challenge to explore. Our ways of life and its innumerable cuisines can be quite an onslaught on our nostrils, especially when it all intermingles. Isolating and following each scent is a game I indulged in. I revelled in the scents of different flowers, crops and vegetation. When walking in the open, I could not run for cover when an offensive smell invaded. I tried to identify animal carcasses in dried-up rivers, molasses, tanneries or clogged drains.

People may find my suggestion—that walking with engaged senses makes us better at our work—far-fetched, but no one can disagree that it makes us more empathetic. I felt like a different person during the 1700. I may have started out from the accommodation grumpily, but I was transformed as I began walking. I found myself always smiling and my hands joined into namaste innumerable times a day. It was like the whole journey was a large jigsaw puzzle and different experiences from each day were the pieces that were coming together to give me messages about the complexity of our country's problems and the simplicity of possible solutions.

Why am I so fixated on the senses? I'll attempt to answer.

Undivided attention to our senses, exclusively experienced, helps sharpen and nurture each sense. While walking, this heightened awareness helped connect me to the here and now. It made me more perceptive, a skill that is essential in the profession of design, but equally important in any other field. A specialist in medicine may find clues on why certain diseases afflict specific pockets or specific groups of people; a marketing executive may understand what drives people's choices; a scientist may be helped with her research as she watches the people make and use dyes in a home-based cottage industry. After all, Newton is supposed to have stumbled upon the concept of gravity while resting under an apple tree, presumably after a walk!

Walk,
and you shall see.
Walk,
and you shall hear.
Walk,
and you shall smell.
Walk,
and you shall feel.
Walk,
and you shall do!

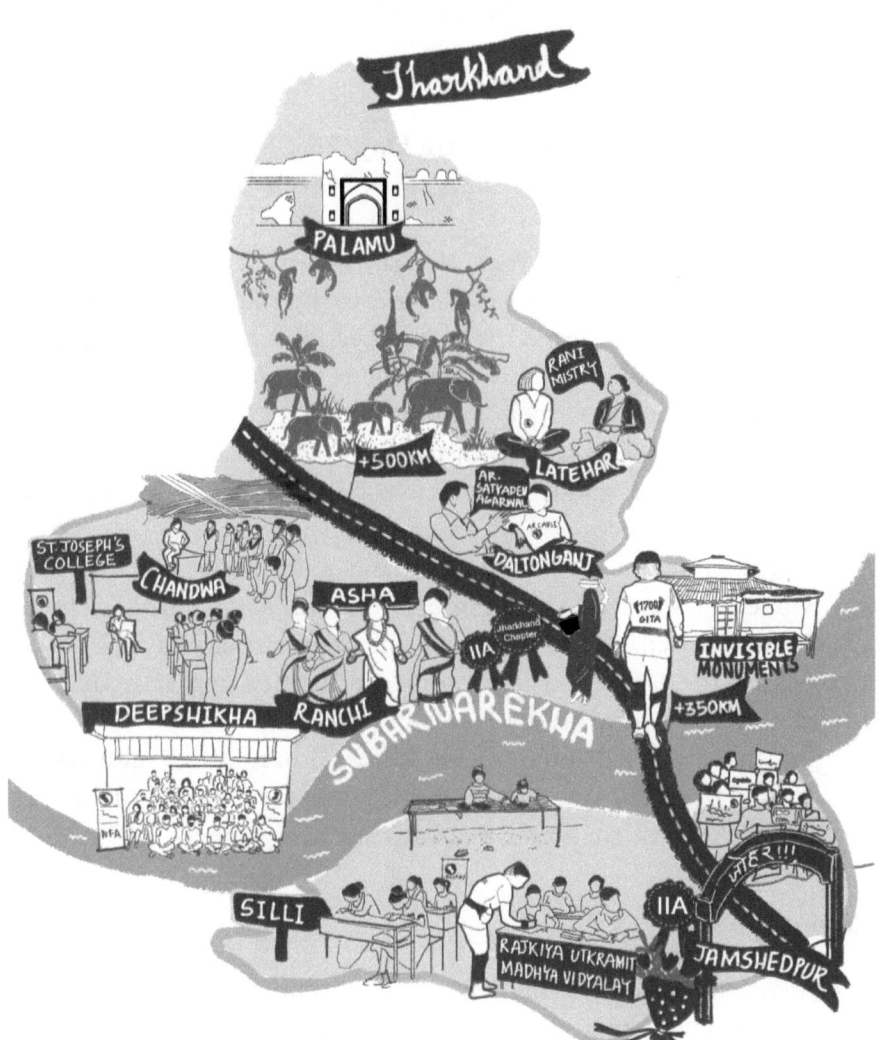

CHAPTER 13

JOHAR IN JHARKHAND!

Day 13 to Day 25
25 February 2022 to 9 March 2022

From nomoshkars in West Bengal, I crossed over to johars in Jharkhand. The 'Johar—Welcome to Jharkhand' sign spanning across the road alerted me to this beautiful greeting. We heard it every day that we were on this land, where people traditionally revere and believe in nature as their primary heritage. Johar is a salutation that calls for complete surrender to nature with faith that this will result in communal good. Does that sound familiar to exhortations for sustainable practices and lifestyles of today?

Johar is a simple daily reminder and a wake-up call that rung true while I walked and ran through the Amjharia Ghati, went on a safari in the Betla forest while the monkeys menacingly teased me by blocking the stairway to my room and women and girls sang and danced their way into my heart.

The Jharkhand Chapter of the IIA organized many interactions including a beautiful one at the Association for Social and Human Awareness (ASHA), an NGO in Namkum near Ranchi.

Showstopper 8

ASHA works with the children of brick kiln workers. Brick kiln workers live away from their villages for almost 8–9 months a year. Their children either go along with them, in which case their education suffers, or they are left behind under the care of some relatives in the village. ASHA steps in to bridge this gap and takes care of these children through its four centres in Jharkhand. ASHA also directs attention to the rights of women and children, with a special focus on tribal communities.

We reached ASHA's premises on an overcast evening, where we were received with garlands of marigolds. The girls were dressed in traditional green and red attire and looked rather chic with their black slip-on shoes. The place wore a festive look and had been set up for our visit.

A whiteboard stood in one corner, and I was pleasantly surprised to find a sketch of me in my walking garb—a fine likeness too. I thanked the young female artist. We walked in and heard a melodious song accompanied by dancing, and I was better prepared this time when they roped me into their circle. Just as we settled down to watch more performances in the front court of the premises, the skies opened. It was a loud downpour. The children were mighty disappointed that their carefully laid out plans had been disrupted. Hence, we gathered indoors and learnt about their lives and returned to the singing and dancing once the rain let up.

I was curious to understand what made their eyes sparkle despite their difficult lives. From our conversations, I understood that ASHA and Mr Ajay Jaiswal, its founder, in particular, had had a big role to play in their happiness. The way the caretakers encouraged interaction between the children and the joy they seemed to find in doing things together left a lasting impression on me.

Showstopper 9

Sumari's original name was Somwari, traditionally named after the day of the week that she was born on, which was Monday or Somwar. This spunky girl decided that she preferred Sumari to Somwari. I posed a question to her about her future plans, and it makes me smile even now when I recall her response. She perfectly articulated that she wished to pursue geography in college because she was interested in rivers, soil, trees and fossils and wanted to learn more about our earth and its treasures. Johar indeed! If only everyone choosing a vocation or embarking on any new venture could have such clarity of purpose!

Anurag Kumar, a Ranchi architect, had arranged for me to visit Firayalal Public School, where all senior school students assembled to hear me speak about 'Design as a Career'. Some students were so interested that they even came on stage to engage in some problem-solving and this demonstrated that I had succeeded in raising their curiosity levels. I followed this up by spending time with the teachers discussing their current homes and also future plans that some had of constructing their own homes. I was happy to see the difference that Haneet Munjal had brought to the discussion, being an architect and a member of the management committee. I left smacking my lips at the precious box of laddoos that I was gifted.

The Council of Architecture engaged with the local architects through Ar. Prashant Sutaria of Mumbai on the roles and responsibilities of an architect. Prashant also shared in detail with the local community the nuances of building a robust architectural practice.

The spirit of Jharkhand's Johar was evident in the enthusiasm evinced by the local community of architects. Over 25 of them joined me at different points as I was heading out of Ranchi and moving towards Kuru; they walked and ran long distances with me. At least three of them kept me company the entire distance. We stopped for our break amidst the rocks of Ratu and I ate my sandwich while they ate some aloo puri. I had been dreading the hot weather and was happily surprised by a sprinkling of rain, a thunderstorm and extremely pleasant conditions for a walking picnic.

I had ended my walk the previous day inside the cantonment area. When I reached there the next day at 5.30 a.m., I grew concerned to find that the area had been barricaded for the general public. I had a 3.7 km route within the cantonment to complete and was in a fix. On speaking to the security guards, I was asked to wait for their supervisor. Once he arrived, I was mildly amused as I found myself negotiating with Javed Miandad, the supervisor and namesake of a well-known Pakistani cricketer. He was extremely cooperative but he only allowed me to enter and Dhanraj to follow on his bike.

I reached my starting point and ran from there to meet the rest of the architects who had decided to walk with me that day. I waved to Javed Miandad as I ran past his post.

At the end of the day, as I neared Kuru, the community of architects bade me a fond farewell. They followed the rest of the 1700 virtually, and one of them coincidentally drove past me on his way to a site visit in Daltonganj the following day. Another memorable interaction I had was at St. Joseph's Rural Community College, an NGO run by Father Alphonse in Chandwa, Jharkhand. He took me to the campus where the NGO ran programmes for young girls from all over Jharkhand, training them to become nurses. While we had danced at ASHA, we sang together here, and I chatted with the trainees about the selfless profession that they were entering into. At the end of the conversation, it dawned on me that only one of these 25-odd girls had actually visited a hospital. They would do so soon as they were about to complete their training and were on the verge of being posted at different hospitals. I comprehended the enormity of the challenge ahead of them: coping with their first job while being away from home and also being entrusted with the daunting responsibility of caring for the sick; they also had to contend with a scale of operations completely alien to them. I wondered, 'Could we include modules on the layout of their place of work during their training?'

Chandwa proved to be an amusing memory for other reasons as well. The lodge we chose was a recently constructed one and named 'Celebration'. On hearing of my record feat, the owner of the lodge offered their best room to me, which happened to be the honeymoon suite! I found myself awake the whole night staring uncomfortably at a rose-shaped velvet pillow next to me. I also remember being all ready for a shower and finding that there was no tap head. I tried all possible manoeuvres to turn the tap without the head but failed and had to step out and call for the boys who were managing the place. One of them casually walked in whistling, took a tap head out from his pocket and fixed it. Apparently, these are removed and stored for safety as they are the items that are pilfered most often. And after all, this was a new establishment waiting to make its mark! I have used the word 'hotel' often in this book. While the word may conjure up lavish images, the many little anecdotes hopefully also convey the modest nature of these accommodations that became our abodes.

Daltonganj, now called Medininagar, got its name from an Irish anthropologist, Colonel Edward Tuite Dalton, who was the commissioner of Chota Nagpur in 1861. It was renamed Medininagar after Maharaja Medini Ray. The town is still abuzz with folklore about the Maharaja. The new fort built by Raja Medini Ray and the old fort built by the king of the Raksel dynasty in the seventeenth century stand as silent testimonies to all the wars that were waged and the different armies that attempted to pass or actually passed through its gates—Akbar's, Jahangir's and the British East India Company's regiments. The new fort was actually never completed as planned by Raja Medini. Although both the forts are in different stages of ruin, they attract visitors as they lie close to the Betla National Park.

As I was running into Daltonganj, I was tickled when an old man on a scooter stopped me and expressed concern about why I was running alone through the busy streets of this ancient town. He offered me a ride and nearly fell off his scooter when he heard that I was on my way to Delhi. Such offers of help came my way in a few other places too, with auto drivers and bus drivers asking me to hop on.

But it was only Day 21. I was already feeling the harshness of the sun as I crossed the Koel River. I had a long way to go to get to Delhi.

I ended my walk in Daltonganj in search of one of the oldest serving architects of this region, S.P. Agrawal. As we interacted in his living room, he spoiled me rotten with sweets and savouries and even a gift—a copy of the *Ramcharitmanas* I will treasure all my life. Unfortunately, he has passed away since and I am grateful to him for having enriched my journey through our fleeting encounter.

As I walked through the undulating terrain of Jharkhand, I often felt like the Pied Piper because I seemed to draw the curiosity of children of all ages. We happily chatted as we matched each other step for step.

I recall one young man, probably a young teenager, Sujit, who told me that his father was a construction worker as we passed the site that his father was working on. He related to what I had to say about the role of a designer and insisted in responding in English, saying 'Yes!' to most of what I had to say, coupled with a naughty twinkle in his eyes. These rendezvous with children over the 70 days never failed to rejuvenate me, and they also helped strengthen my resolve. I wanted to keep engaging with them actively as they are the most receptive at this age. The exposure that students in remote government schools receive is very limited; the vocations that they hear about and that seem attainable to them are restricted to teaching, the armed forces, the police forces, nursing, driving, construction work and the like. They need to be exposed to a multitude of other possibilities and our education system needs to be made amenable for them to fit into and achieve career paths of their choice with no encumbrances. The path of education really needs to be inclusive and must provide equal opportunities for all. Currently, the marginalized are also marginalized in their choice of careers. While some of them continue to pursue higher education, language becomes a barrier too huge to overcome. Also, design (as a profession) keeps marching on an elitist path! Designers who grow out of some of these regions may actually be the answer to development on the right track, provided that our design curriculum also undergoes drastic changes to mandate contextual learning.

I also fondly recall meeting a bunch of schoolgirls. I waved to two girls travelling with an older man across the road, and as is my wont, told them that I was on this walk from Kolkata to Delhi. They waved back and I walked on.

Around 500 metres ahead, I saw a group of girls from classes 5 to 9 waiting for me under a temporary shed on the roadside. One of the girls was actually jumping up and down while beckoning for me to stop. The girls I had met earlier were also there. The man was their auto driver who ferried them to school. We sat together chatting until it was time for them to head to class. I was mighty impressed with the level of openness and curiosity displayed by these children. They wanted to know everything and asked me a number of questions! When I bid them farewell, I wondered where life would take them. Where would it take me?

CHAPTER 14

ACCLIMATIZATION

Acclimatization is the process or the result of becoming accustomed to a new climate or new conditions. Challenges of physical endurance, such as mine, undertaken while focusing on a mission, are not taken on by too many. I did not know of many people who could advise me. After all, each body is different, as are reactions to external stimuli.

Acclimatization is a word often used by architects and designers, but this took on a whole new meaning as I travelled in temperatures ranging from 25°C–13°C to 43°C–27°C. While I had trained and prepared myself by strengthening my lower body and my core, I could not fathom the impact that clocking a mileage of 25–35 km almost every day would have on me. The first couple of weeks were hard. My limbs would throb even as I slept. Then I gradually learned new exercises and the importance of ice and cold water in the process of recovery; I also discovered the simple magic of elevating my legs as I rested. While I had practised a lot during my training for this walk and my earlier runs, the actual agony that these activities could render unfolded as I walked the 1700. The use of compression socks was advocated strongly and I ordered them online, but our moving from one place to another resulted in them reaching me in three weeks. Meanwhile, we managed to purchase football socks in Ranchi and the team cracked jokes at my expense as I sported canary yellow and parrot green socks until the compression socks of a more sombre colour reached me.

I travel a lot for work. Despite this, staying away from family and familiar surroundings for such a long duration had not been a part of my experiences so far. Thanks to video calls and good connectivity, I was able to tune into what was happening in the lives of my family members and friends, and they were able to tune into mine. I had the on-ground team with me (Vinayak, Param, Shantanu and Dhanraj) and they became my family on this trip—but even that needed getting used to. Getting to know their lives, their struggles, their aspirations, their interests and knowing about the people they love became important to me. This made our small conversations more meaningful. I adjusted to their eccentricities as they adjusted to mine.

Param was the youngest, with the least travel experience, but showed the maximum enthusiasm in wanting to make the most of this trip. Shantanu and he made a great team while capturing the journey. Vinayak and Dhanraj shared the burden of ensuring that we had a place to stay, left on time, our planned interactions went as per plan and anything I needed was handled. I worked on laughing at their jokes, listened to music they suggested and discussed the movies they liked—although watching the movies *Pushpa* and *KGF: Chapter 2* was something I could not bring myself to do. We did watch *The Kashmir Files* in Rewa though. The team needed to get acclimatized too. They were coming together for the first time and needed to share rooms and even beds with each other. We discovered who the loudest snorer was, and soon there were jocular comments on how the ecstasy of someone could be the agony of another. Group dynamics also needed to be taken into consideration, and regular team meetings ensured that things went well. We bonded as a team and I was relieved that being on time was a top priority for everyone. However unearthly the hour I chose to set out, they were always ready and waiting.

I am only comfortable in my own bed with my own pillow. I cannot sleep in another room even in my own home and I get acutely distressed when I have to use a toilet other than the one attached to my bedroom. The last thing that most women do before leaving home is empty their bladder—we are all too aware and sceptical of the sanitary conditions of the toilets we may encounter outside our homes. And here I was, having to negotiate with a different bed every day, with bathrooms and food nowhere close to what I was used to.

However, not once on the 1700 did I grimace at the state of our accommodation or the toilets that I had to use! I felt no concern or revulsion within me either. This was probably acclimatization of the highest order for me. I made sure to eat simple and light meals; dessert became a rare luxury. Strangely, I found no craving for any kind of food and was happy with what was available. It was certainly sad that local cuisine was something I rarely found in restaurants, which only served what people did not make at home, such as dishes with rich gravies, cottage cheese, Indian Chinese fare and the like.

The road was long and hard. I left my room every morning not knowing what terrain and weather I would encounter. Walking similar distances on a daily basis in familiar environs is a very different experience from walking through the unknown. Acclimatization on the 1700 meant building tenacity to adapt to the unexpected, on the go, every minute of the way.

CHAPTER 15

POLITICS IS LIFE

My route took me in and out of Uttar Pradesh three times, and I entered it at Wyndhamganj, Jhansi and Kheragarh near Mathura. I felt a warmth when I was first welcomed in Uttar Pradesh, and that had me thinking that the original plan of walking through this state would have been a good idea too, elections notwithstanding.

Speaking of elections, I was walking to Renukoot on the day the election results were announced. Bharatiya Janata Party (or the BJP), which is the ruling party at the centre, had swept the elections. I had sensed this mood even before the results had been announced. Casual conversations indicated to me the direction the wind was blowing in. It was sheer coincidence that the bandanna I sported on the day of the results was orange, which perfectly matched the many similar coloured turbans, flags and kurtas that I encountered. I grasped this only after the sun had risen when I could see sloganeering people in small lorries and bikes. They felt a sense of kinship with me. I cringed awkwardly as I am not someone who wears my political heart on my sleeve. But Renukoot and Uttar Pradesh were in a celebratory mood; music was blaring and people were dancing while distributing sweets freely.

Every election in India, be it the general or state elections, reveals that the turnout in rural areas and smaller towns is typically far higher than that of larger urban settlements. It was evident to me that the rural areas had a lot more at stake and also felt the impact of government policies more sharply. They were a barometer of the performance or the non-performance of initiatives and schemes. Hence, politics mattered and they wanted to play their part in electoral dramas and verdicts.

There were many who openly proclaimed their party affiliations and were also quite vocal about which party had the upper hand and discussed why, too. There were those who were curious to know about my political affiliation. Seeing the West Bengal registration plate on the accompanying car, I was asked about the state of affairs in West Bengal in comparison with the states I was walking through. There were times when I was asked to take a message for the administration back where I was walking from. There were those who asked me if I was planning to launch a career in politics and hence this walk, echoing what some of my city friends had voiced as well. I was happy to see no apparent animosity in these conversations. We do hear of disagreements, unrest and even riots during electoral campaigns but from these interactions, it seemed to me that seeds of discord are sown by politicians in order to stay relevant.

Showstopper 10

Many erstwhile royal families retain their relevance through a career in politics. I did visit the home office of the MLA of Nagod, Nagendra Singh ji, and what a bustling office it was! The MLA is over eighty years old, and was super active; he met people, had formal meetings and travelled to areas in and around his constituency. I was told that he would start his day at 4 a.m. and continue working into the late hours of the night. His cousin and he have been in active politics for most of their lives, and he has alternated between the roles of a minister, MP and MLA for fifty years now!

I met his family and it was interesting to see how openly the pros and cons of initiatives and action areas were being discussed. The locals were waiting for their turn to meet the MLA and share their woes or seek blessings for a happy event in their lives. The MLA patiently heard them and dispensed solutions to some on the spot as well.

On another occasion, members of the opposition party in the area I was in accosted me and we discussed the role of the opposition in a democracy. I walked through many political events where local leaders, ministers and even a chief minister were hosting events and rallies.

All this was educational for me. I do follow politics intensely, but here I was, learning the art of viewing the political landscape from the lens of the most affected, and in a sense, the most powerful too. I understood why political parties spend so much time in villages with the intention of winning villagers over. Every so often, city folk have misjudged the pulse of people and have analysed governance and development only from the urban perspective. Undoubtedly, migration has resulted in an increase in the urban population, but India still lives in her villages. This became increasingly clear to me.

I recalled attending a talk by Peter Scriver about his book, co-authored with Amit Srivastava, *India: Modern Architectures in History*,[16] where he maps the political and economic development in different countries over time through the evolution of architectural styles and trends. As I moved from one state and one village to the other, I also moved constantly from one political stronghold to the other. I did not need anyone to label this for me. The graffiti, slogans, the verbal posturing of people even in simple conversations, hoardings, advertisements for political events, etc., were all giveaways. I also came across so many pockets—groups of homes or villages—that seemed prosperous, but within them, there were a few zones that seemed rather neglected. Who you owed allegiance to decided how you did in life. I wished ours was a just world, where once the elections ended, good governance for all took over until the next campaign!

---

[16]Scriver, Peter, and Amit Srivastava, *India: Modern Architectures in History*, Reaktion Books, Islington, London, 14 October 2015.

CHAPTER 16

ZIGZAGGING THROUGH UTTAR PRADESH!

Day 25 to Day 30
9 March 2022 to 14 March 2022

I never imagined the welcome I would receive as I entered Uttar Pradesh. It was a day to remember.

I bid farewell to Jharkhand after taking a few selfies with the cops stationed at the border. I ran into Dudhi Tehsil of Uttar Pradesh, past all the trucks halted at the border. It so happened that a man (with his infant) at a roadside tea stall stopped me to satisfy his curiosity. When he heard of me and my mission, he grew mighty excited. Gradually, a crowd of around 150–200 people gathered around me, wanting to know more and keen to help. The tea vendor nearby offered some tea, and I could not refuse (though I do not drink my tea with milk and sugar). I was overwhelmed by the affection from this throng of strangers. Virendra Kumar, who had initially accosted me, was also a part-time local reporter and he conducted a quick video interview. The following day, news about me and my walk had found its way into close to half a dozen newspapers.[17]

Smaller media houses and the vernacular press were receptive and large-hearted in their coverage. I could sense familiarity in the nods, smiles and stares from people along the way. It was not uncommon for people on bikes to halt and ask for a picture with me, and within minutes, I was tagged on social media. Many followed my journey and were rooting for me till the very end. My 'Walk for Arcause' was

---

[17]*Digital Bharat News, SNC Urjanchal, Janpad News, Son India News* and SBN, to name a few.

spread over sixty pieces in different newspapers. Most of them were unsolicited!

As I made my way through the Dudhi, I felt a strange sense of belonging when I encountered small groups of people waving to me along the way. After I ended my day and was doing my stretches on the roadside, two men alighted from a scooter and beamed at me with huge smiles on their faces. On closer scrutiny, I realized they were Virendra Kumar and Dharmendra Gupta—men I had met that morning—all cleaned up and dressed for work. They were advocates and were really keen on taking me to their workplace. Instead, I negotiated with them and asked them to take me to the abandoned church they had referred to earlier. They were quite excited by my request and led the way on their scooter through the winding lanes of Wyndhamganj.

Showstopper 11

I saw the old church completely in ruins; gnarled tree branches were hugging the structure and making it quite inaccessible. We met the caretaker, Ibrahim, who informed us that there were no plans to revive the building and that the church that owned it had no funds. The story we were told about an old British man living in this building complex made his grand life from the past flash before our eyes. In close proximity was another well-maintained, quaint and simple church. This is the functioning church and it serves the 800–900-strong local Christian population. Ibrahim, a Muslim man, is the caretaker—a testimony to the beauty of the plurality of India! I actually asked for his name twice to be sure I had heard right. I had already witnessed many such examples: sights of a Pandit sitting with a Moulvi reading their own newspapers while sipping morning tea at the neighbourhood shop; temples sharing their compound wall with mosques; sounds of the azaan mingling with bhajans in the wee hours of the morning. These were all poignant reminders of peaceful coexistence. Nonetheless, I have to admit to reading many slogans that evoked a different reality.

The landscape transformed as I marched from Dudhi to Renukoot.

I climbed up and down hilly roads, moving from a regular small town and tehsil to a totally industrial township. Renukoot is a part of the Sonbhadra district and is known for its aluminium factories. These factories were set up in 1963 by G.D. Birla at Jawaharlal Nehru's request when they both visited Renukoot for the inauguration of the Rihand Dam.

I entered Renukoot on the day the election results were to be announced. Traffic had come to a standstill. All mobile lines were jammed.

My team was scattered. I took a mud route through the desolate interiors of Sonbhadra. I walked close to 10 km on muddy tracks. I was also largely alone on these stretches as the vehicles could not follow me. A railway line was being laid on this stretch and there were no trees or shelters on the way where I could rest my feet. I soon ran out of water and any form of nourishment. With no connectivity, I could not even be sure that I was moving in the right direction.

As this was an important day for the region, there was no work on the railway track underway either. There was no one in sight for kilometres. The dusty roads and the hugely uneven surfaces made it extremely difficult to keep a reasonable pace. I even had to cross large slushy craters.

I realized that I had to keep my wits around me. I had always known that there would be days like this. This was the second such day so far. I had already experienced physical stress when I had to trudge through undulating fields and cross culverts on one stretch on the way to Ranchi. But this was certainly far tougher. I muttered affirmations to myself and drew on my inner strength. I strategized that in order to find my way to the nearest town or village, it would be best for me to follow the railway tracks that were under construction, and that is how I reached Renukoot station. Once I was reunited with my team there, I got to know that they had been watching me from a higher vantage point over the last couple of kilometres. We all heaved sighs of relief and moved on to find a place to stay.

We had a lovely interaction with teachers that evening. It was organized by the Lions Club of Renukoot. Every teacher had a garland of marigold flowers for me and I felt overwhelmed by their affection.

These interactions made me look forward to the next day.

I was also visited by the members of Banwasi Seva Ashram, an NGO that abides by Gandhian principles. They run a large campus where they cater to issues faced by the forest-dwelling communities, especially the most vulnerable, through capacity-building and innovative development plans. Thanks to the torrid day, my plan to visit their campus had to be abandoned, but I am fortunate to have met these beautiful people. As they left, I promised them and myself that I would certainly visit their centre someday.

A few members of the Lions Club evinced interest in joining me the next day as I walked down towards Sonbhadra district. Over the past few days, others had made such promises but had not kept their word. I thought I would be walking alone this time around too. The next morning, I had barely walked 3 or 4 km when Gopal broke the jinx by joining me with great enthusiasm. He had his car follow him, but he walked and ran almost 10 km with me. He told me about his life, his family, about how he and his brother were businessmen and that fitness was his hobby. As we crossed some truck drivers sitting on charpoys at a tea stall, Gopal was stopped by them for a chat. After a while, he came running up to me, his eyes twinkling with mirth. The drivers had interrogated him in amazement and curiosity because they had passed by me in Daltonganj a few days earlier and they were seeing me here again, striding away.

Thoughts about the lives of these truck drivers had often been on my mind during my journey. While mine was a journey of a lifetime, their journeys were their lifeline. Their trucks were an extension of themselves.

I had come across so many of them every day on this trip, awake at unearthly hours. Some were likely to have set out to deliver material to nearby cities and towns and had to leave early before the restrictions on city and town roads kicked in. Others were on longer journeys, transporting automobiles, goods, food items, fuel and so much more. I thought of the similarities between their journeys and mine. They were constantly on the move, resting in a new place, meeting new people every day. The messages on the rear of these trucks bring smiles to many travellers. In sections of Uttar Pradesh and Rajasthan, the trucks were decorated in a riot of colours and were an expression of art. The musical horns in these parts brought cheer, almost as if the vehicles were talking to one another. The blaring music from some trucks brought on a lightness to my journey as well.

Many dhabas (eateries) along the way put out charpoys at night for truck drivers to sleep on. I even saw an interesting dormitory of sorts made of bamboo and thatch with a reception area for truck drivers to check in and rent one cot from a row of them! Many of these dhabas had sheltered migrant workers who were trudging back home during the lockdown. The truck drivers too had likely saved many lives by transporting people at the cost of serious personal difficulty and disruption.

Day 47 to Day 49
31 March 2022 to 2 April 2022

After three days in Renukoot, we were in Madhya Pradesh, only to enter Uttar Pradesh once again at Jhansi. Jhansi is known all over India for the fiery queen, the Rani of Jhansi. Born into a Marathi family as Manikarnika in Benares (now Varanasi), she spent her childhood learning fencing, shooting and equestrian skills with her friends—Nana Saheb and Tantia Tope—breaking all stereotypes attributed to women. Radical for those times certainly, but she's still a role model for many today. She was married to the Maharaja of Jhansi, Gangadhar Rao Newalkar, and took on her new name, Lakshmibai. After the death of the king, the British, under the Doctrine of Lapse, wished to annex Jhansi—their excuse was that her son was merely an adopted heir. She fought valiantly to her death to resist the British onslaught and played a crucial role in the Revolt of 1857. As I climbed up the ramparts of the Jhansi fort, the scenes from the *Amar Chitra Katha* comics I read as a child played out before me.

Balwant Nagar is the old name of Jhansi that sits on the banks of Pahuj River and is a part of the Bundelkhand region. My walk through the town of Jhansi was short and sweet. I entered the Jhansi district near Mauranipur, which is said to be the largest tehsil in India by land area. This town was known in ancient times as Madhupuri.

Because it has a large sprinkling of temples, some locals refer to it as mini-Ayodhya. The route took me through thickly wooded terrain, which brought the temperature down by a few degrees.

Showstopper 12

My narrative of Uttar Pradesh would not be complete if I did not speak of my visit to a government school in the village of Bangra in the Jhansi district. The smart young teacher, Preeti, lived in the nearby village, Luhari, and she took care of her four-year-old son and infant—who came along to school with her—while managing to engage all the students actively. I saw a happy bunch of students, eyes sparkling with a thirst to learn. My presentation, 'Learning from Nature', was an instant hit here. I heard sighs and saw expressions of wonder from the students in the class.

I must also mention Kapoori Devi Yadav, one of the three Anganwadi workers assigned to this village, along with Kalpana Devi and Parvati Devi. Kapoori Devi's husband and son are farmers and Kapoori herself started as an Anganwadi volunteer in 1983, eight years after the launch of the Anganwadi program in India. She has been a health worker for four decades now. The three of them are responsible for advising villagers on matters of health and nutrition. They particularly attend to women, pregnant mothers and infants because Kapoori believes that if you educate a woman, you educate a family. Kapoori even sang a few songs and rhymes to spread awareness and keep children busy.

Day 62 to Day 67
15 April 2022 to 20 April 2022

Uttar Pradesh kept playing hide-and-seek with me. I left the state only to enter it again at Kheragarh after a short stretch in Rajasthan. Kheragarh is a simple border town that too needs some attention. People here began encouraging me, saying there was less than 250 km to go! I walked on from Kheragarh, eagerly reaching Mathura where the G.L. Bajaj Group of Institutions hosted a grand welcome for me at their college. I attended some stimulating interactions with the young students there.

As I made my way out of Uttar Pradesh for the final time, I paid a silent ode to the Jhansi ki Ranis of today—Kapoori, Kalpana, Parvati and Preeti. It is champions like them and their dedicated service that have set India on the path of awareness and positive change.

CHAPTER 17

A TALE OF TWO CITIES

We moved to Delhi in 1982 when I was in Class 10. Our first abode, until we moved to our home, was the Lodhi Hotel, very close to Mathura Road. All through my eight years in Delhi, we came across Mathura Road quite often. The significance of the name never occurred to me then—this was a road that connected Delhi to Mathura! I then recalled the roads (named after towns they connected) that I walked on this trip—Purulia Road, Ranchi Road, Panna Road and Khajuraho Road, to name a few.

I was on Mathura Road. The salutations of 'Ram Ram' gradually changed to 'Radhe Radhe' and 'Hare Krishna' on the way from Morena on the outskirts of Gwalior. Here, Brij Bhoomi begins with Mathura, with Vrindavan as its spiritual centre. Brij Bhoomi is considered a holy place for worshippers of Lord Krishna who, according to scriptures, was born in Mathura while his beloved Radha was born in Barsana, also in this region. Brij Bhoomi extends on two sides of the Yamuna and covers some parts of Madhya Pradesh, Rajasthan, Uttar Pradesh and even Haryana. This portion of Uttar Pradesh is well marked out and different religious circuits are followed by pilgrims. The '84 Kos Yatra' is equivalent to a 252-kilometre circuit and is the most preferred route of many pilgrims. Along my route, I came across pilgrims walking to different temples as a fulfilment of a vow. There were some who had vowed not to walk but to locomote only on their hands, buttocks and soles of their feet. In the scorching heat, they had to use cardboard pieces under them to shield themselves from the heat of the metalled road surface. I marvelled at their tenacity and their devotion.

There are many legends associated with this region. Govardhan, the mountain that Krishna lifted on his little finger to provide shelter to the region from rain and floods, is a part of Mathura. Krishna's birthplace was a prison where the ancient Kesava Deo temple was situated and is now marked by a temple complex. Mathura was an important commercial hub in ancient times, falling on a prominent caravan route. The etymology of Mathura reveals that it comes from 'Madhuvan' and then 'Madhupura', named as the area was a thickly wooded region (a 'van'). Excavations dating back to the sixth century BCE have been found in this region. However, there is hardly any evidence of the forest this region once was today.

Barely 15 km from Mathura is Vrindavan, its twin, where Lord Krishna is supposed to have spent his childhood. 'Vrindavan' can be translated to a 'forest of tulsi,' a sacred shrub for Hindus. The Radha Madan Mohan temple at Vrindavan is one of the oldest and most popular sites on the pilgrim list. While passing through Vrindavan, we also visited the Prem Mandir, a more recent temple inaugurated in 2012—and evidently so. Prem Mandir is designed to dazzle, hoping to enamour those who like glitz and flamboyance. The building and the artefacts around it were on show and colourful lights completed the panorama. Huge crowds thronged the place, but those who wished for quietude would find it hard to ferret out a refuge in this complex.

The fact that Vrindavan alone has over 5,500 temples is enough for us to realize that religion rules here. Religion is inseparably woven into every facet of life in Mathura and Vrindavan. Religion here is a collective quest. Lives, vocations and professions revolve around the calendar of festivals, religious tourism and auspicious dates. All temple precincts have informal and formal shopping areas. Symbols invoking Radha and Krishna are omnipresent.

Param, Dhanraj and I went on a two-hour boat ride to savour the sights along the river as well as to see the Yamuna Aarti along Vishram Ghat and learnt that 'Krishna' is probably the most common name here. We were not surprised when our oarsman responded with 'Krishna' when we asked for his name. Vinayak had to handle an emergency—our missing car keys—and hence did not join us. Fortunately, after a nightmarish search, the keys were found lodged in his sock, but how it found its way there is a mystery to date.

It was a pleasant evening and the breeze brought down the soaring day temperatures. The river's calm flow soothed me immensely and I sensed an ethereal character to the evening. The aarti at the Vishram

Ghat started promptly at 7 p.m. with claps and chants from the devotees. The structure was a candyfloss pink, and the aarti being performed within its bright yellow pavilion turned out to be quite a sight. It was like we had a gallery view! There were many other boats around us, and the oarsmen were principled in giving way to allow all boats to have a view. Krishna, our oarsman, told us that Lord Krishna is supposed to have rested at these ghats after slaying his cruel uncle, Kamsa. Locals also believe that Krishna used to play the flute on the branch of a kadamba (or burflower) tree.

On speaking to Krishna, we learnt that our oarsman was a college student and he rowed as he believed he was taking people towards the God that they loved. He said that it also kept him fit and he did not need to go to a gym or do any other exercise. He had ambitions of attaining a government job after graduation and was aware that he would lose his proximity to the river once he moved to another city. He averred that his spiritual connection with the flowing water would always help him in the flow of his life's journey.

Mathura, well-known for its sweets and confections, is a paradise for sweet lovers and prasad hunters. Uttar Pradesh ranks first in the number of sugarcane farms and accounts for almost 50 per cent of India's total cane farms.[18] The state also has almost as many sugar mills as Maharashtra, which has the highest in the country—and this was evident from the number of flies that I had to contend with during the walk. The buzzing around my face had started well before we even entered Uttar Pradesh for the last time.

As we were exiting Mathura, I chose to walk through the busiest areas at the busiest of times—the evening bazaar. This was an area with rows of sweet shops, and the smell of milk cakes and sweets being fried in ghee wafted in and saturated the air around us. Although I had decided not to eat any sweets during the last two weeks of the trip, walking through this street satiated my appetite. Weaving my way through people walking, rickshaws and bicycles, I emerged onto the quieter outskirts of Mathura. I had achieved my highest mileage for a day on the trip—40 km!

---

[18]Farmers' Portal, https://www.farmer.gov.in/. Accessed on 23 November 2023.

Top: *A grand welcome into Uttar Pradesh at Wyndhamganj*
Bottom: *En route to Renukoot*

Day 30—Walking through the Singrauli Coalfield in Madhya Pradesh

Day 30—In front of the Jeevan Rekha Express (or the Lifeline Express), then stationed at Majholi in Madhya Pradesh

Top: *Scaling the ever-changing terrain at Rewa in Madhya Pradesh*
Bottom: *Day 37—Exchanging folklore with a temple priest on the banks of the Tamas River in Madhya Pradesh*

Top: *Day 38—With students of Blooms Academy after a session on 'Design as a Career' at Satna in Madhya Pradesh*
Bottom: *Day 44—Casual conversations with the locals while en route to Chhatarpur*

Top: *Day 48—Being welcomed by Guddo at TARAgram, an organization that supports the growth of sustainable employment in rural areas at Orchha in Madhya Pradesh*

Bottom: *Day 49—Children racing towards me to show their art after a fulfilling drawing and colouring workshop conducted at Santa Maria Azad Community School at Orchha in Madhya Pradesh*

Day 51—Harshvardhan Dubey, a gifted music instructor, didn't let his impaired vision stop him from pursuing his passion at Datia in Madhya Pradesh

Stretching post-walk

CHAPTER 18

TOILET TALES

M any who later heard about my walk had an unspoken question written clearly on their faces, 'Where would she relieve herself?' The import of the term 'relieving oneself' hit home the most on this trip. On several days, I had to use bushes, culverts, abandoned construction sites and old buildings to empty my bladder. I confronted a reality that is an impediment to making India open defecation-free.

The team was relieved and I too would smile in gratitude when I saw a board for a petrol bunk, even if it was still 8 km away. I knew that in about 70–80 minutes I would be able to empty my bladder, hence I spaced my liquid intake accordingly. The idea of having toilets and washrooms in petrol bunks was thought up by someone sensitive for sure. It is indeed laudable that it has become a part of planning policy in our country and, more importantly, is being enforced and adhered to well. Often, we found that the petrol bunks kept these toilets locked, particularly the ones for women, to ensure sanitary conditions. As these toilets were open to all and sundry on the highways, I was rather surprised that many of them were reasonably well-kept. I always made it a point to thank the bunk employees as I left. There were times when the toilet's condition completely surpassed my expectations and I did go up to the management to compliment them for this essential service.

But wait! I was not always walking on highways. And not all highways had petrol bunks at even 30-kilometre stretches, which was my average daily walking distance. Also, I had to keep hydrated in view of the soaring temperatures and the extent of physical activity. When the temperatures were lower (when I started the journey in February), I needed at least three, and sometimes even four loo breaks during the six to seven hours that I was walking. As it got warmer into March and April, I could do with one or two toilet breaks. But there were many days when we did not come across a petrol bunk for the whole walking distance, and we would often not come upon one when I needed it most. The first time I used a clump of bushes a little away from the roadside was akin to an achievement. My team became my set of bouncers, keeping watch while I quickly completed my job. Once it was done the first time, it was as if some kind of barrier had been broken. I grew comfortable and began using abandoned buildings, sites with high boundary walls, and of course, the ubiquitous vegetation and the rocky outcrops that were sometimes available, as and when needed. I was wary of insects and snakes though, and am fortunate that I did not have any such unfavourable encounters. I usually woke up an hour before setting out, and my intake of dietary fibre was crucial to ensure morning bowel movement. Since I began my walk while it was still dark every day, I came across many who used the cover of darkness to empty their bowels in the fields. Women went out in small groups to stay safe. There were sections where I noted the vegetation and the biodiversity and realized that there could be snakes and other creepy crawlies; hence, spaces closer to homes were used by these women. Apart from the lack of dignity, this has resulted in unhealthy living conditions too.

Over a decade ago, I met Dr Shyama Ramani, an economist from France who grew to become a friend for life. She set up the Friend in Need India Trust and dedicated many years of her life to building Ecosan toilets in the village of Kameswaram in Tamil Nadu. The village was affected during the tsunami of 2004.

She invited me to conduct a workshop for the local masons and that was my first introduction to her project. I was later invited as a judge for the 'Toilet Beauty Contest' and this turned out to be a delightful experience. I thought to myself, 'What an idea!' Instilling pride in this possession is key to ensuring that it is used and maintained! So many of us take a toilet, a basic necessity, for granted, but it is actually a luxury for a large proportion of people in our country. At the beauty contest, the denizens of the village showed me around their toilets, the accessories they had added and the messages they had painted on the toilet walls to educate the rest of the village on sanitation.

During my walk, I also had the opportunity to use the facilities in the welcoming homes of different villagers. As is the custom in India, the toilet is still considered the most unsanitary part of a home and is positioned as a separate self-standing unit in many rural homes. It is often a trudge away from the main house, especially where farms or a yard are a part of the compound. Many of these units did not have latrines; there was merely a hole in the wall for the urine and the water to drain out. These bathrooms were often without a roof or had just a tarpaulin or a cloth cover, and women primarily used these toilets.

Showstopper 13

One such toilet I used belonged to Rajua, a resident of Umari village in Madhya Pradesh. As I got out of the toilet, I was amused to find Rajua waiting with a band of women. She held my hand and said I had to pay her a fee for using her toilet. She led me through a lane to a site where she was constructing her new home. The foundation had already been laid and she wanted tips from me on improving her home. She wanted me to tell her if she had planned it right. I paid my fee in the best way I could and was back on my way.

Rajua's niece, Chandni, had pointed me to the toilet. She was returning from fetching water for a day from a couple of kilometres away, walking her cycle, which had containers of water straddled on its handle. I struck up a conversation with this bright-eyed young college-going girl. This chat and many others along the way revealed the complexity of attaining the United Nations' sustainable development goal of clean water and sanitation, which aims to make the world open-defecation-free by 2030. We often hear statistics of the number of toilets that have been constructed in villages through government schemes or by NGOs, and we also hear of people lamenting about these rooms lying in disuse or being used as just another room by those they were built for. I have heard this being attributed to a lack of awareness. It is certainly not as simple as that.

Besides cultural dictates and norms, the issue is one of economics as well. I was told that if one uses the fields, only one lota (a quantity equal to a mug) of water was required to wash oneself. But the water required to maintain a toilet is a lot more—a minimum of two buckets per person per day. In some of the regions I passed by, water was indeed a precious commodity. If Chandni had to bring more buckets of water to keep the toilet clean, it would mean that she would spend an additional couple of hours on this chore. In such contexts, wouldn't it make more sense to build community toilets with community water sources and encourage a community management system as well? I recalled my time at AVAS in Bengaluru, working at the slum at Baiyappanahalli, where such a system had been adopted and was effectively managed by the slum-dwellers themselves.

Showstopper 14

There are some people who come into your life for a reason. Sunita Devi, a female mason I met in Latehar in Jharkhand, was one such woman. She showed me how one can build one's life, mission and livelihood, as well as develop empathy. She is a social worker...a crusader...a woman who worked against all odds to spread awareness regarding the importance of sanitation. As a woman, she realized the difficulties women face in this respect and took to building toilets as a woman contractor and a mason. She underwent government-supported training on building twin-pit latrines and made this her mission. As she went around building toilets, she realized that the pits in many of them were slightly smaller than intended because of the thickness of the pit walls. At times, the rim of the pit was slightly above or below the ground level, which caused problems of its own. Sunita Devi made alterations to the measurements and design to avoid issues of maintenance that sometimes made the toilets unusable.

Ours is a large country with varied lifestyles and cultures, and it is necessary to devise approaches and plans that align with ground realities. The design of the toilet unit itself needs to undergo changes based on the location it is meant for, and these need to be developed in consultation with the people of the area. This is one way to ensure that the toilets that are built by government agencies and different NGOs are actually put to use.

I saw many buses stopping in the middle of nowhere for a toilet break for the passengers they were ferrying. While the men crossed over to the other side of the road, the women rushed to the fields, bushes or trees on the same side of the road where the bus had stopped. I marvelled at the design of the saree in its different avatars and even the ghaghra (long skirt) or the dhoti the men adorned. They would squat comfortably and complete their job without revealing any part of their body. I had told my team before we set off that circumstances may arise when raincoats (which we were carrying for emergencies) would have to play the same role. During my saunters around different cities and towns, as I prepared for this walk, my visual and aural senses told me that there was a desperate need for toilets near bus stops where passengers completed their long travels or prepared for one. These are simple cues for planners to keep in mind while designing public spaces.

A toilet in a home can change lives. People should not need to control their intake of water and food during the day for fear of needing to relieve themselves. Every home usually has elderly, infirm and sometimes bedridden family members; even a temporary illness is easier to manage with a toilet at home. A toilet can mean security and safety for the womenfolk of a household. A telling story was how the construction of a functional toilet in their house meant that Babli, a blind girl, could now be left in the safety of their home, and her grandmother could then set out to earn her livelihood.

But why should Babli not be able to wander out safely and find her way around herself? That is another story.

Walk,
in hope.
Walk,
in faith.
Walk,
with empathy.
Walk,
with belief.
Walk,
and you shall resolve.

CHAPTER 19

PITY IS NOT EMPATHY

Day 51
4 April 2022

Showstopper 15

I had just reached Datia, a historical and bustling town in Madhya Pradesh. My back-end team had arranged for me to interact with a person with visual impairment, Harshvardhan Dubey, through the NGO, Shri Vansh Gopal Lok Kalyan Samiti. We met a representative of the NGO at the Pitambara Peeth temple and drove to the locality where Harshvardhan lived. I was not in a particularly good mood; I was tired and had not managed to complete my routine of a cool down and stretches. To add to it, finding Harshvardhan's home was proving to be a challenge. Finally, Vinod Kumar Mishra, a family friend of the Dubeys, who also turned out to be the convener of the Indian National Trust for Art and Cultural Heritage (INTACH), Datia Chapter, appeared on his bike. I hopped onto his bike and we reached the destination.

We were received by a young man who guided me to the first floor of the house. He opened a room and requested me to sit on the mattresses that were laid out. He turned on the fan and brought out his harmonium and said that he would like to sing for me. I was a little perturbed and wanted to finish what I was there for. I confessed to him that I was more interested in meeting and chatting with Harshvardhan first. He broke into a broad smile, saying he was Harshvardhan, the person with visual impairment that I was in search of!

Completely perplexed, I asked him how he had navigated the space with such ease.

His response was a telling commentary on the sorry state of affairs with respect to making spaces accessible. His house was familiar terrain, and moving around within it was something he had mastered. But the minute he moved out of his home, he needed to be chaperoned and there was no place where he felt welcome. We do not really need to do an in-depth study to understand what he was referring to! Our public spaces, sidewalks and other street furniture, surfaces and textures of floors and walls, location of stairwells and elevators, the slope of ramps, visual aids and signs or the lack of them all tell a story of extreme apathy.

My sons studied at Akshar, an inclusive school in Kolkata. I still remember my first visit to the school after we had moved to the city from Bengaluru. As we were waiting outside the principal's office to be called in, a girl with Down's syndrome walked over, took Pranav by his hand, and gave him a tour of the school premises. That really sealed our decision of wanting our boys to study and grow at Akshar. I strongly believe that this certainly helped our family members become better human beings.

Over the years, I have perceived a complete lack of empathy in the way people with disabilities are treated by society and also in the way spaces are planned and designed—or not designed—to be inclusive. We see people feeling sorry for persons with mental or physical disabilities, helping them cross a road, or completing a chore for them. I have tried to put myself in their shoes and see that these actions would dent my dignity. Pity is not empathy.

I came across a park named 'All Ability Park' as I was running along the promenade in Visakhapatnam a few months after the walk and it made me happy because the very name is inclusive. I do hope the park is for all to enjoy equally as per their ability. My mind travelled back to the day I met Harshvardhan and I resolved to make Universal Design one of the key pillars of Ethos Foundation.

Showstopper 16

When I met the charming Gopika at Deepshikha, an NGO in Ranchi, I was informed that she was the Miss Wheelchair India runner-up in the year 2013. She had lost her mobility in an accident. I recoiled when I heard that there was actually a Miss Wheelchair India event! Does the beauty, wit and charm of someone differ if they're wheelchair-bound? But then, I also understood that it was this event that strengthened her resolve and empowered her to voice her concerns and to work towards building awareness of the need for inclusive planning.

Organizations such as Deepshikha instil hope, and I am glad that I was introduced to it by Atul Saraf, an architect from Ranchi. Sudha and Alka are the main movers of this thirty-five-year-old organization and they have been serving the cause of building dignity and self-reliance in people with disabilities with great sensitivity. Discussions on policy, on the need to make universal accessibility an intrinsic part of the architecture curriculum in colleges ensued during my visit. Students and faculty members of the architecture department of the Birla Institute of Technology, Mesra, were present and actively participated in the interaction. The need to renovate the premises to make it amenable for people with different disabilities to navigate it with ease was expressed. At the same time, it was felt that the building should perform well from the viewpoints of space organization and well-being. This was a project for a fellowship on a platter! I was determined to make this design project a reality and a fellowship was announced a few months after my walk, in collaboration with the School of Architecture, Carnegie Mellon University, IIA Jharkhand Chapter and Atulya Architects. Sai Uphad won the fellowship and completed the first stage of redesigning the premises to make it a model centre for people with disabilities. This has paved the way for the actualization of a dream once Deepshikha raises funds for the execution of the project.

Inclusivity requires that we address the needs of all, irrespective of ability, age, gender, class or creed. Design and designers can and should play a huge role in filling the crevasses that exist in this realm. In many Western countries, we see the ease with which wheelchair-bound alight a bus or move around. The design of the wheelchair, roads and surfaces, pavements, the foldable ramp that replaces the steps, the interior of the bus with its earmarked space for the wheelchair, the anchoring of the wheelchair when the bus moves and, most importantly, the attitude of people, all need to come together for a wheelchair-bound person to be able to get on a bus with dignity. Signages in Braille in the recently launched Vande Bharat Express is a baby step in the right direction.

Siddhant Shah started 'Access for All' and made it his life's mission when the need for such an intervention came to his attention on seeing his mother lose her eyesight gradually. Do we need to witness the suffering of someone in our families or that of someone close to us to wake us up to the reality that diversity needs to be embraced and accessibility needs to be universal?

CHAPTER 20

THE WOMEN OF MY COUNTRY: THE OTHER HALF?

The female population in our country in 2020 was 662.9 million against the male population of 717 million.[19] Observing women and drawing inferences from my daily interactions about their position in society became an important pursuit for me on the 1700. I was not looking at producing a factual research paper but was instead getting a first-hand perspective on women's place in society. Interestingly, these observations threw up insights on a lot of other fronts too. Women hold varied positions—while they seem to wield a lot of influence in determining choices that families make, they are marginalized when making critical choices in their own lives. For instance, they do have a say in the kind of home they would be building, where the kitchen and the toilet should be, the number of rooms, the sizes of the rooms and even financial planning, but they lose their voice when decisions on their daughter's education, marriage or their own desire to start a business or begin a vocation is in question. There are unsaid norms and rules that are in play all the time that not many dare to confront.

On construction sites, people were surprised when I asked why women were paid lower rates. No one had a response, but no one expected the question either. There were many worksites where there were no women in the construction workforce. I was consoled by friends in Jamshedpur who knew of contractors ensuring parity as they found great value in the sincerity of the women on their sites. I was

[19]'Gender Ratio in India', *Statistics Times*, United Nations, 27 November 2023, https://statisticstimes.com/demographics/country/india-sex-ratio.php. Accessed on 4 January 2024.

also happy to hear the verdict that better well-being was ensured on sites where men and women worked together. Women architects too are more likely to be accepted on sites where there are construction workers from both sexes and gender parity is practised.

I saw women on their way to work in fields and construction sites—taking healthcare to doorsteps, running errands, handling shops and much more. I came across many instances of sisterhood through simple actions. A woman rushed to help me thinking I was injured when I sank to the floor in exhaustion. There were many women who wanted me to look at their homes and to have tea with them. One old woman casually asked me to help her with a load of firewood that she was trying to lift onto her back. While it was certainly a photo opportunity that we missed, it is so cleanly etched in my mind. She did not think twice before asking me—almost as if I belonged. I bonded with women around a well; as they were drawing water, they spoke of their miseries about not having a water source near their homes.

There were women who walked together to a neighbouring village to work in the fields and were paid for their labour in the form of the grains harvested from the farms. It was lovely to see them, a group of colourful ladies sitting on the side of the road, chatting happily after having a breakfast that they had brought from their homes. They were waiting for 9 a.m. when they would start toiling in the fields. They did not think they were being exploited by not being paid any wages. What they got in return for their hard work helped them tide through the period when there was no work on the farms.

The transformation in habits and behaviours across different states and even within regions of the same state was quite drastic. Women in West Bengal and Jharkhand appeared less inhibited; they rode bicycles as a common mode of transport. I even saw a few women carrying men as their pillion riders. Young girls in trousers were not an uncommon sight in the rural areas of these states. While women in most parts of West Bengal were very friendly, I saw a certain reticence in their demeanour as we reached Purulia, possibly reflecting the stress owing to the impending elections. I felt an infectious vibrancy in the young girls in Jharkhand and hoped that they would be able to retain it throughout their lives. Women were garrulous in Uttar Pradesh and

Madhya Pradesh, but some of them were camera-shy. The ghungat (veil) was a regular feature I noticed once I left Jharkhand behind. In Madhya Pradesh, an old lady refused to believe that I was walking this whole distance. I gave up trying to convince her that it was true and humoured her.

The girls I walked with at Madla in the Panna district of Madhya Pradesh were special; they had an answer for every question and a question for every answer. While they excitedly told me about their future plans, I heard a young man sniggering in the background. He said, 'All their future plans will be decided by their better halves.' While his comment echoed reality, I hoped that seeing me venture out had given them some courage to prove the man wrong. With access to information being more even, I am sure these young girls have enough role models to emulate those who had risen from the most nondescript places like phoenixes.

I saw women and children in the Sonbhadra belt, collecting blocks of coal that fell off plying trucks, big and small. The research paper 'From Gin Girls to Scavengers: Women in Raniganj Collieries' written by Kuntala Lahiri Dutt[20] records the plight of the Adivasi community and women from other lower castes of Raniganj who worked in the coal mines until they were gradually eased out as a consequence of mechanization. And then, more recently, I read about Shivani Meena, the first woman excavation engineer to work in an open-cast coal mine, following closely the achievement of Akanksha Kumari who became Coal India's first mining engineer.[21]

I encountered my own share of champions on this trip. Women who were strong but gentle, who were achievers without even knowing it, who were aggressive but full of kindness, who were dreamers steeped in reality. At Champadanga, West Bengal, Mitu and Reena had gone incessantly from door to door during the pandemic, spreading

---

[20]Lahiri-Dutt, Kuntala, 'From Gin Girls to Scavengers: Women in Raniganj Collieries', *Economic and Political Weekly*, Vol. 36, No. 44, 2001, 4213–4221.
[21]'Coal India Welcomes First Woman Excavation Engineer', *The Telegraph Online*, The Telegraph, 10 September 2021, https://www.telegraphindia.com/jharkhand/coal-india-welcomes-first-woman-excavation-engineer/cid/1830164. Accessed on 4 January 2024.

awareness, ensuring proper care was given and quarantine procedures were followed. Working at a resort in Joypur, Anjali proudly spoke of her home built using traditional construction practices, though part of her felt compelled by modern construction. Together with Mita, Pakhi, Bandana and many others, Anjali told me about their work at the organic farm and vegetable garden at the resort, which generated employment for the local populace in the region. In Madhabpur village, the womenfolk had organized themselves into a self-help group with the support of Mallabhum Prayas, an NGO, to jointly cater to the issues of the village and to garner support for collective initiatives. A young and jubilant Sumari from Ranchi wanted to study geography as she understood and felt attached to her land.

These women will stay with me forever—Rajua, the single parent and construction worker in Umari, Madhya Pradesh; Kapoori Devi, the Anganwadi worker in Bangra; Sanchita, the fiery leader of the NGO in Gwalior; Sunita Devi, the rani mistry in Latehar, Jharkhand; Lali, the old widow in Palwal, Haryana, who completed the '84 Kos Yatra' pilgrimage; and Jasodha, the maternal figure in Rajasthan. These are all women of substance, and India has so many of such women.

Luke Easter, a baseball player, is known to have said, 'A strong woman knows she has strength enough for the journey, but a woman of strength knows that it is in the journey where she will become strong.'

Women are planners, doers and leaders, all in one, and so transformation in our country is being led by women. Many government schemes, whether it is the 'Beti Bachao Beti Padhao', 'Kanyashree' or 'Ujjwala', have certainly helped change the lives of quite a few women. These women have, in turn, influenced many more to take decisive steps in improving their own lives and consequently the lives of those around them. I have heard about Ganga Ahirwar, a woman from the Muhalpur village of Guna district, who used the Ajeevika Mission to better her own life and that of her family. She then went on to start the Uma Self-Help Group with eleven women to further the impact. There are many such Gangas in our country making waves quietly. They may be unsung heroes but their voices are loud hymns of change.

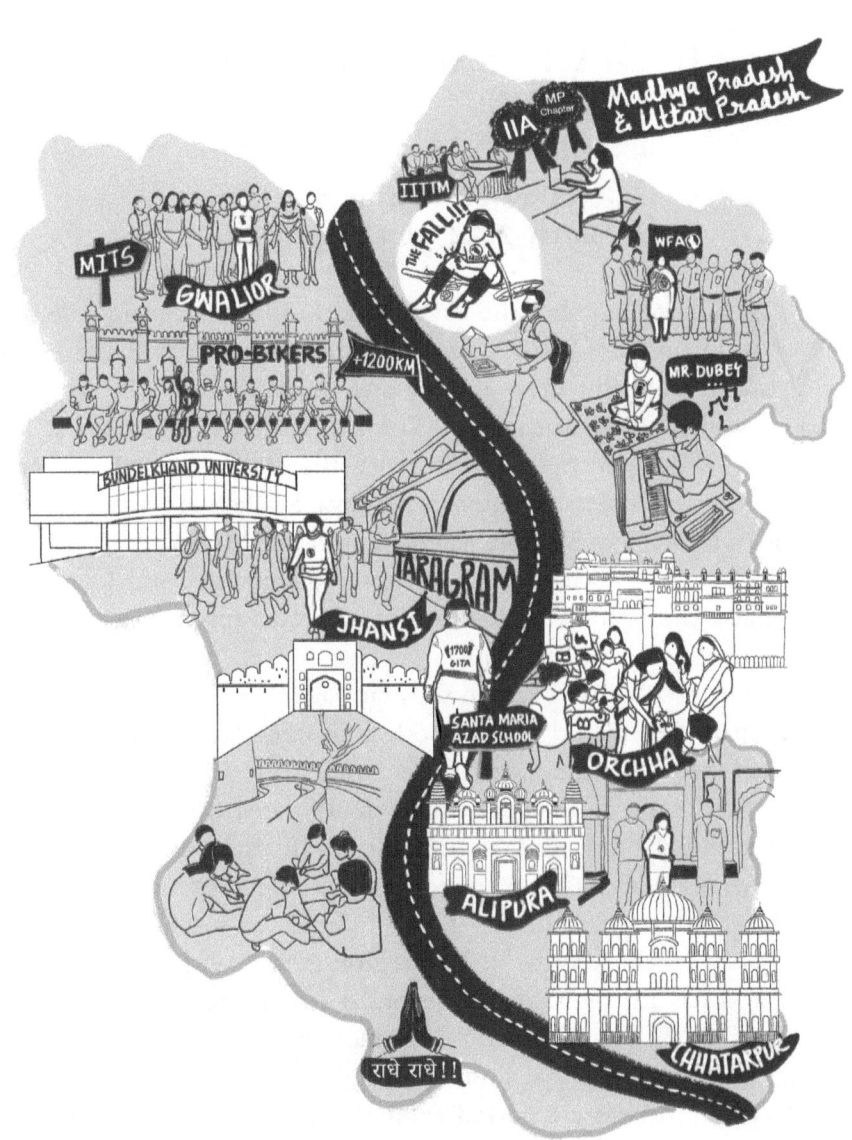

CHAPTER 21

INDIA IS LARGE-HEARTED

Day 29 to Day 59
13 March 2022 to 12 April 2022

Madhya Pradesh is the largest state in India, covering 3,08,000 square km. When I was working on my route, the allure of this state drew me, despite the additional 250 km that I had to walk to cross through it. The magnitude of the state at the heart of India dawned on me only when the 700 km that I traversed through seemed endless. I entered Madhya Pradesh on Day 29 and exited it only on Day 59. The segment through Madhya Pradesh was 40 per cent of the total journey in terms of distance, and I had not even walked through its widest section. I relate this to give you an idea of the expanse of this state.

My visits to Madhya Pradesh thus far have been limited to Bhopal, Indore, Ujjain, Pench and Sanchi, both as business trips and for leisure. Panna had been on the cards for a while, but it never happened because there is no direct accessibility to the area from Kolkata; one has to travel via train or take a flight to Jabalpur or Gwalior and drive down 214 or 302 km, respectively. In light of the fact that I had not visited Panna because it was difficult to reach, the irony is that I walked all the way to it! The region is rich with its forests and wildlife and has its fair share of historical structures.

Thanks to Major General S.S. Kahlon who was then posted in Kolkata, I connected with Shyamendra Singh, also known locally as 'Vini Raja', even before I started from Kolkata. My stay at Panna was to be my big vacation.

Showstopper 17

We stayed at the Ken River Resort owned by Vini, a wildlife and agroforestry enthusiast who had turned into a hotelier and started the resort in 1986. This was the time when initial attempts were underway to make wildlife and environmental conservation economically sustainable through tourism. Many more resorts and homestays have sprung up in the vicinity and now, together with the wildlife reserve, they provide employment to the local community, hiring them as hospitality staff, guides and naturalists. The river Ken, originally known as the Karnavati, flowed quietly as I continued my walk during the day on three of the five days that we stayed at this resort. Dining and watching the river from the tree house was quite rejuvenating after a hard day's activity.

Showstopper 18

While Panna was to be my big vacation on the 1700, it was quite busy too. There were a lot of things on the itinerary. I visited an NGO called PashooPakshee where girls from the local village, Madla, were being trained to enhance their skills and then assigned projects that helped them earn their livelihood. I later learnt that this project had come to an end when I went back to Madla on another trip, months later. These sprightly girls showed great enthusiasm when I asked them if they would like to walk a few kilometres with me. That plan was then sealed!

Close to a dozen young women from Madla and a class of bubbly children from Maharani Durga Rajyalaxmi School in Panna waited for me at a designated spot as I ran down the slopes from Panna to Madla to complete that segment of the journey on foot. The girls from Classes 11 and 12, dreaming up careers that they would like to pursue, were exposed to design as a possibility as they matched me step for step.

Madhya Pradesh, and Madla, in particular, certainly enriched my journey. Madla manifested great potential for my future plans for the foundation.

This did turn out to be the first Ethos Foundation Fellowship to get off the anvil in collaboration with the local community and Hunnarshala Foundation—Gaurav Chordia won the award. Seeing pictures almost a year later of Gaurav's interactions with Madla, its people and its environment brought back a flood of memories of a glorious stay.

Showstopper 19

Khajuraho was also ticked off my bucket list as it was just 24 km away from Ken River Resort. As we sauntered with our guide, Narendra Kumar Sharma, around the complex of temples built by the Chandelas, I wondered how this place would have been if it actually got its name from the date palm trees that were said to have been plentiful in this region. The guide kept us engrossed in stories and histories of this place and its people, breathing life into the intricately carved panels. The intense and vivid descriptions of the erotic friezes painted a picture of a way of life that would not be considered normal today.

While there were other tourists, I understood from the locals that the number was not even a fraction of what they were used to. The pandemic had played its part in making this place look like a ghost town for a period of time—it was as if time had paused, they said. Hospitality, transportation services, tourism-related shops and more operations were hugely affected. There was a relaxed spirit in the demeanour of many people now that the pandemic was seeming to retreat and tourists were returning.

I entered Madhya Pradesh through Singrauli and the four days it took to cover Singrauli were probably the most gruelling of the 1700. The pandemic was not a concern and wearing masks was not a necessity, but the air on the highway was high in coal dust and I had to wear a mask to protect my lungs. It turned black in no time. I looked quite a few shades darker just by having walked a few minutes, and my t-shirt and shoes carried vestiges of the coal dust till the end of the 1700. All that my eye could see was covered in dust—leaves, thatched huts, hoardings, vehicles, everything.

To add to my misery, all the roads to Sidhi were in a constant state of repair or disrepair. The plight of border towns stared at me once again. The roads rarely had a metal surface, and the dust from trucks ferrying coal had settled on the road. My feet sank an inch and sometimes more on these dusty roads. A line of trucks would often pass by me, kicking up a huge dust storm that I would be enveloped in. I do not prefer sunglasses because I do not enjoy the unreal tint that comes with them. Over those four days, I wore dark glasses to save my eyes from the dust.

But these days were also among the most memorable days of my trip. Walking through a part of the country that supplied power to the states of Uttar Pradesh, Uttarakhand, Rajasthan, Punjab, Himachal Pradesh, Chandigarh, Delhi and Jammu and Kashmir was again a reminder of how far we had come since Independence.

So much in Madhya Pradesh held me in raptures. From Sidhi, the road and the infrastructure became among the best. My route took me through Rewa, Satna, Nagod, Panna, Chhatarpur, Nowgong, Alipura, Datia, Orchha and Gwalior before we left the state. The entire route was dotted with muted monuments—living heritage of common people in different shapes and sizes, dating back to different points in history. They seemed to belong to their surroundings. On the contrary, the newer 'builtscape' belonged neither to the past nor to the present and appeared to be highly out of place, threatening with tacit aggression to destroy any semblance of a local vocabulary or identity.

It would be remiss of me not to laud the MP Tourism hotels that we found all along the way. These were cheerful, bright and well-kept places to retire. The staff at all these places were extremely courteous and helpful. I stayed only at two of them, but it was apparent that the standards were upheld across all the properties. State assets need to be maintained and also need to be business-worthy to survive and thrive, and MP Tourism has certainly managed to do so!

Beyond hotels and lodges, the hospitality in Madhya Pradesh was visible in its villages, its people and the community of architects. Small towns have so few architects that they can be counted on the fingers of one hand and yet they came together. The IIA, MP Chapter, led by the then Chairman and Junior Vice President, Ar. Jitendra Mehta and senior architect Sanjeev Bumb, respectively, received me in Rewa and continued to engage with my journey in the state with events and interactions being organized in Rewa, Satna, Chhatarpur and Gwalior until I left.

Showstopper 20

On the advice of a local architect, Raviraj Parihar, I visited Art Ichol in Ichol village of the Maihar district of Madhya Pradesh, a creative retreat for artists, writers and sculptors and the brainchild of Ambica Beri, an art arbiter, a connoisseur, a Calcuttan. Although there were no artists there during our visit, I felt their souls in their creations and it made this campus come alive. As you enter Art Ichol, a life-like sculpture of the architect, Suraj P. Subherwal, Ambica's father, greets you. God bless his soul! He is known to have spent over two years in this nondescript village to fulfil his daughter's dream, and Art Ichol has certainly put Ichol, even Satna and Maihar, on the tourist, art and design map of the country and the world. Every piece of art spoke to me and told me a story of its making.

Some installations moved me immensely. There was a tribute to the brick; a material that the artist believed was going to become extinct soon. I also noted a project of empty packets or pouches of snacks; the project helped keep the entire village clean and created interesting patterns of floor coverings, wall art, etc., with this waste material. There was a bronze sculpture of Baba Allauddin Khan at the sarod under a mango tree, and I almost heard the Raag Manj Khamaj as I meandered among these different installations. Baba is said to have hailed from Bangladesh, and he became one with the heart of India—and his story is melodious, carrying songs of diversity in our country.

Gyanendra Gautam, the young caretaker of the complex, was earlier an electrician on the project, and he won over the hearts of the artists and visitors and also was won over by the idea of Art Ichol. He is now passionately involved in the well-being of the place.

Showstopper 21

Many of the towns and cities that we crossed were on their way to becoming 'smart' under the Smart Cities Mission of the Government of India. Among the lot, Satna stood out for me. The roads were wide, and neatly planned bicycle and pedestrian paths were laid and colour-coded. Signs had been planned with care and the local sensibilities were maintained in the colours and the graphics.

But people will be people! We still found cyclists and pedestrians on the roads.

Another energizing interaction was organized by Blooms Academy in Satna with young students on the brink of making their career choices. One of the young boys there aspired to join the armed forces and we spoke of Pradeep Mehra, another army aspirant who was filmed running on the roads of Noida at midnight by filmmaker Vinod Kapri. Before embarking on the 1700, I read *1232 km: The Long Journey Home* by Kapri that narrated the travails of seven migrant workers who set out on bicycles from Ghaziabad during the first lockdown caused by the pandemic to get to their hometown Saharsa in Bihar, a distance of 1232 km.

It goes without saying that we also discussed architecture and design as possible career paths. One young man had me in splits when he innocently asked me if I had been nervous that I would not be able to answer their questions.

Showstopper 22

As I neared Rewa, I saw what appeared to be a large body of water. I wondered why the ambient temperature had not reduced. When I got up close, I realized it was a sea of another kind. I was at one of Asia's largest 750 MW solar power project. While I knew the site would be on my route, I was not prepared for the magnitude of this renewable energy initiative—the Rewa Ultra Mega Solar—dedicated to the nation by Prime Minister Narendra Modi in July 2020. The entire solar park covers an area of 1,590 acres—this may help you gauge my wonder. This is the first solar project in India to break the 'grid parity barrier', a term I learnt from this project. Grid parity indicates that an alternative energy source is generating power at a cost lower than or equal to the price of power from the electricity grid. Projects like this filled me with hope and pride about our country's achievements and abilities!

Showstopper 23

My tryst with the Lifeline Express at Majholi in Madhya Pradesh was an experience that left me delighted at the simplicity of the response to the huge problem of making quality healthcare available to people who needed it the most. Started by the Impact India Foundation in 1991 and strongly backed by the government and Indian Railways, it is a powerful initiative that takes healthcare to the doorstep of remote villages. Railway coaches have been refurbished to accommodate operation theatres that can handle surgeries of the eyes, ears and teeth. Accommodations have been designed for 27 staff members who travel from village to village over the year, and there is space for a kitchen for meals to be cooked for the travelling staff and the visiting doctors. The arrival of the train was celebrated by the local village folk, and the railway station of Majholi underwent a quaint makeover as the train was parked for the month of March to serve the region of Bargawan.

Thousands of patients are scanned in a makeshift OPD by local government doctors, and those who need surgery are referred to the surgeons on the Lifeline Express. The speciality of the surgeons volunteering is dependent on the nature of complaints in that village. This Express has been in operation for over two decades and has touched many lives. The idea of using trains for isolation chambers during the pandemic was triggered by the Lifeline Express.

I shook hands with Rupesh Shetty, who was managing the on-ground initiative at Majholi and walked away from the operation theatre on wheels, dreaming of a day when design would similarly be made accessible to those who need it most.

Showstopper 24

Another initiative, on a completely different scale, evoked great nostalgia and assurance in me: TARAgram in Orchha, a successful experiment by Development Alternatives launched in the year 1995. Many of my contemporaries have used this site as their training ground during graduation and immediately after graduating as architects. Touring the different projects, I understood why this was such a fertile ground for learning.

There was a handmade paper-making unit churning out reams; women were working their magic on these sheets to transform them into marketable products as per placed orders. While they were able to pull out the damp sheet of pressed paper with skill and ease, they watched with amusement when I destroyed a sheet as I tried my hand at their job. They reassured me that the damaged sheet would simply go back into the raw material to be pulped.

I also noticed a vegetable store sporting a board that said '*Imandari Ki Dukaan*' (shop of honesty), which placed the onus on the buyer to be fair. It negated the need for anyone to supervise and manage the store. The paper-making unit was run by women, and Guddo, one of the workers, extended to me a traditional welcome with a tika. Guddo had been working at the centre since it began in 1995. She told me that I reminded her of another Geeta whom they had worked with. As people learnt about my visit to TARAgram, I too realized who this Geeta was—Geeta Vaidyanathan, who was then with the architecture department at the Sri Sri University, Cuttack, and had spent a few years of her life at TARAgram!

On a recent visit to the office of Development Alternatives in Delhi, I was heartbroken to hear that Guddo passed away a few months ago. She was an institution in herself and with her passing, a slice of history has also moved into oblivion—the smiles, the laughter and the camaraderie that she epitomized cannot be captured for posterity. I shed a silent tear remembering her energy when she had shown me around.

Later, the students and faculty members of the architecture department of Bundelkhand University toured the TARAgram premises with me and we ended the day chatting with each other over tea and snacks. I was shown a site where building products, such as ferrocement, roofing tiles, pipes and fly-ash bricks, were being made and where textiles and handicrafts, spices and high-value food/medicinal products were also being produced. They largely use biomass and other locally available raw materials for manufacturing their products.

The produced material was up for sale, but the quantities were not sufficient for the market. I then understood that this was more of a unit for demonstration and training. Villagers underwent training here and then went on to use the same process to make their own material as per the requirements on their respective sites. While most villagers there seemed to be aware of TARAgram, more needs to be done to encourage the use of these alternative technologies in the town of Orchha itself!

Showstopper 25

One of my most heart-warming interactions took place at the Santa Maria Azad Community School in Azadpura village. What made it special was that this visit was facilitated by Mrs Annie Koshy, the principal of St. Mary's School, Delhi, my alma mater. She had also been instrumental in setting up this school and introduced me to Pushkar, the principal of the Santa Maria Azad Community School. Besides the school, these premises also served as a meeting place for many of the village women and men. I was shown pictures and videos of women in sarees and ghunghats playing handball among other activities.

Later, the students of Bundelkhand University helped conduct a drawing and colouring workshop for the little children as I interacted with the older children and parents. My interaction was pleasantly interrupted and brought to a close when the tiny tots ran up to show me what they had created. It was an evening to cherish and remember.

The inroads made by the internet, even in the remote corners of our country, were obvious when young girls from the village started following me on social media and posting our pictures even before I had left the village!

The expressways in Madhya Pradesh are certainly well-designed for vehicles. Public conveniences were more frequent and well-maintained too. But those who travel on a bicycle or on foot did not appear to be in consideration. Walking on these swanky expressways, I had enough time to contemplate on the transformation. Thousands of homes had been levelled to make way for this development, and habitation had been pushed deeper. Only farmlands ran alongside much of the length of these roads. Often the villages had moved away from these networks to continue to have their own environs, different from those around these new roadways. At times, I felt that I was walking through a slice of time. It was almost as if someone had taken a saw and hacked through the homes on either side in a straight line to make way for the roadway to go through. Parts of homes were still in use, and the broken-down parts stood open-faced at the road. I would not have been shocked if I had spotted a pot of dal boiling on one of the countertops or if someone had walked out of the doors of these half-houses. The cupboards and shelves still stocked memories. Most of these structures had to be reconstructed, now that the road was on much higher level than that of the floor, sometimes as much as over a storey higher.

The route cut through the rather picturesque Chambal ravines and I remembered how the very name Chambal would invoke fear at one time. This was a time when the lives of Phoolan Devi, Man Singh, Paan Singh Tomar and many more were household tales narrated by the elderly. I felt a sense of gratitude that I was able to traverse these regions with no anxiety.

I then reached Gwalior, which was among the most eventful of stays. It deserves a chapter of its own. Nicknamed 'The Gateway to Madhya Pradesh', it turned out to be my last stop in the state. Madhya Pradesh can satiate every kind of visitor. It dates back to the Palaeolithic age and there are remains from almost every event in history since then, all to be savoured by those interested. The flora and fauna, the rocks and the mountains, the built and natural heritage beckoned me to make another trip—maybe another time, maybe using another mode of transport!

Walk,
and you shall learn.
Walk,
and you shall lose.
Walk,
and you shall live.
Walk,
and you shall deliver.
Walk,
and you shall become.

CHAPTER 22

THERE ARE OTHER RIVERS

*T*here are Other Rivers: On Foot Across India[22] is a book that I read before I embarked on this journey. All the rivers I crossed reminded me of Alastair Humphreys' quest. Heraclitus is known to have said, 'No man steps into the same river twice, for it is not the same river and he is not the same man.'[23] This rang true for me on my journey. Seeing a river meander and make its way is spiritually elevating. When I walked on the Howrah Bridge across the Hooghly River, the western distributary of the Ganga, it was the first day of my expedition on foot and I only felt excited for what lay ahead. By the time I walked from the border of Delhi towards Raj Ghat and crossed the last river, the Yamuna, I had encountered 43 rivers and tributaries and so many more water bodies in the form of tanks, canals, ponds and lakes. I had whispered to some of these waters and wondered about the many lives that had been nourished by them and the lives that had perished because of their tides.

As I sat close to the banks of the river Narmada in Orchha and observed the pilgrims, I recalled Gita Mehta's *A River Sutra*[24] where Narmada is the sutra or the sacred thread that weaves six tales together. Announcements blaring from a loudspeaker made me smile as they alerted me to the beliefs and habits of pilgrims. These announcements advised people to not follow the religious practice of leaving behind

[22]Humphreys, Alastair, *There Are Other Rivers: On Foot Across India*, Lightning Source Inc, La Vergne, TN, 28 November 2011.
[23]Bhaskar, Arushi. 'UPSC Essentials | This Quote Means: "You don't step into the same river twice"', *The Indian Express*, 4 December 2022, https://indianexpress.com/article/explained/upsc-essentials-this-quote-means-step-into-same-river-twice-8304349/. Accessed on 4 January 2024.
[24]Mehta, Gita, *A River Sutra*, Bantam Doubleday Dell Publishing Group, Inc., New York, NY, 1 January 1993.

their old clothes in the river as they donned new ones—the practice was probably symbolic of beginning life anew. Special care was advised for babies that had been brought here to be blessed by the river. The attention that the announcer paid to describing people he was calling out to caution was impressive.

A river in India and in many other ancient civilizations is considered to be sacred and is worshipped. A river can be a lifeline, nurturing its surroundings with its water, allowing for transportation, creating fertile soils and simply bringing solace to the soul. On the other hand, a river can wreak havoc when it unleashes its fury. Both these faces of rivers are why they are so venerated.

There is a lot in a name. The names of these different rivers and waterbodies shared a wealth of information. Sometimes the name reveals the main river to which she is a tributary, like the Adi Ganga. The name of the local deity was whispered through another name, as in the case of Narmada. Yet another got its name from the local folklore of that region, which was Subarnarekha. This river stands out as a happy memory from my journey. It was located at the border of the second state that I crossed into. I stood on the bridge over this beautiful river as Jharkhand beckoned. Legend has it that this river bed was lined with gold and so it has received its name. However, it is likely that the reflecting sun made it appear golden.

Over my journey, I saw rivers that were pristine and rivers that seemed beyond repair. There were rivers with abundant water flowing through them, evoking joy, and then there were rivers whose beds were clearly visible. There were rivers that we actually walked through as they were completely dry; we even smelt the carcasses of animals all around us as we walked through these dry rivers.

Showstopper 26

As I stood taking in the expanse of the Rihand Dam and the mighty Rihand (also known as Renu, Renuka, Rend, Rer and Rehar), I silently thought of the many lives that would have undergone upheaval during the construction of this dam so that many of our lives could be lit. The Rihand Dam is the reason for the metamorphosis of the

Sonbhadra region, transformed from a largely agrarian society into an industrial one, with Renukoot and Singrauli emerging as bustling, busy industrial towns. Sonbhadra was also called the Switzerland of India.

The terrain that I crossed on the day I saw this beauty was all downhill, and I raced down the hairpin bends joyously. The landscape transformed from the busy industrial town of Renukoot to the tranquil natural environs of Sonbhadra. I sensed the conversations between the manmade and the natural as I sojourned through this region. And I heard nature groaning under the burden of the factories and the resultant pollution, issuing constant warnings of impending dangers. I also heard the beautiful dam that had made peace with the river.

CHAPTER 23

A TYPICAL DAY: WHAT IS THAT?

Having started my walk in the pleasant month of February, we set out around 5.30 a.m. from our accommodation and began walking by 6 a.m. as the lowest temperatures still hovered between 13°C and 16°C while the maximum was around 25°C. But temperatures were rising quite rapidly, and by March I was facing a minimum of 20°C and a high of 36°C, which soon shot as high as 43°C as we entered Uttar Pradesh and Madhya Pradesh. When I had planned the dates for the walk and studied the weather patterns, I was to reach Delhi with maximum temperatures touching 36°C–38°C—which would have meant only a couple of weeks of high temperatures. As luck would have it, it was the hottest April in 122 years, and I was walking through scorching heat for most of the journey. Hence, we had to advance our departure time to as early as 4 a.m. within a month, which meant waking around 3.15 a.m. every walking day of the trip (5–7 days a week).

I would pack my required snacks and nourishment the previous evening. I would lay out my clothes, bandanna, wristband, socks and the two belts—one to carry my stash of snacks and the other for my phone and earphones—at night. During the 40–60 minutes I had before we left, I would finish my ablutions as soon as I could and fill my bottles with hydration fluids needed during the walk and after. And then it was time to get on to my mat for pulsing stretches and a routine with the foam roller. I would finish this regimen and join the team who would be ready and waiting, having loaded the car. On days that we were checking out from an accommodation (once every two days on average), we would load the big bags into the car at night to save time in the mornings. The car would then ferry me to the starting point, which was the end point of the previous day. The duration we had to drive usually varied between 5 and 45 minutes. However, we had to drive up to 90 minutes on some days to get to the start point—like the time we stayed at Bharatpur—away from our route. Before I began the walk, I once again did gentle stretches and some brisk warm-up exercises before setting out into the dark.

On a journey like this, no day is typical. You may be doing the same things over and over but every moment of each day is different. There is no feeling of déjà vu whatsoever. The aches and pains are also different. I had to rein in my temptation to break into a run as I started walking. When I had started training for the walk, I had already realized how difficult it would be to stay on my feet for so long. In the last month of my training, I began walking on alternate days and, on the other days, I sprinted for 300 metres and walked for 700 metres. This helped me continue my interactions, brought variety to my activity, directed my attention to the immediate kilometre and not to the full distance and alternated the use of different muscles.

The first hour of walking in the dark was one of contemplation—one where the rhythm of my strides in the silence and the solitude brought serenity to my breath and calmed my mind. I felt the power of the Brahma Muhurta and looked forward to this hour every day. I was growing addicted to the sight of the sky lighting up gradually, coloured in different shades of blue, red, pink and orange as the sun rose every day. The colours depended on where I was walking, the temperature, humidity, pollution levels and sometimes, I believe, even my state of mind. As I was walking westwards most of the time, the sun rose behind me and I would turn around and stop to savour the sight. It never failed to bring a smile to my face. This moment every day was worth living for, I thought. I was reminded of Forrest Gump saying, 'And then in the desert, when the sun comes up, I couldn't tell where heaven stopped and the earth began. It's so beautiful.'[25] And yes, I did watch *Forrest Gump* again on this journey.

These couple of hours were also a time of heightened sense of awareness. I was sensitive to the differences in temperature, the

---

[25]Forrest Gump is the fictional lead character of the 1994 American comedy-drama film *Forrest Gump* directed by Robert Zemeckis and written by Eric Roth.

changing sounds (from quietude to chaos), the smells of bonfires on early winter mornings or the pungent smoke from people burning their rubbish. I experienced what we had studied in school—the temperature dropped just around sunrise and I used this time to quicken my pace before the heat got to me.

As I revelled in the sunrise, I would begin to chant affirmations and allow memories of people who are part of me and my life, even those who have passed on, to float into my mind. I would do this for the next hour until it was nice and bright enough for me to start connecting with the people on the route—women on their way to fetch water, men on their way to their farms, people with *datun* or neem chew sticks, the traditional toothbrushes. The lota had been replaced by ubiquitous plastic soft drink bottles for their morning ablutions. It was heartening to see morning walkers from different sections of society, of different sizes and ages too. It appears that the pandemic had spurred them into activity! What are the chances that a couple I catch up with in Sidhi in Madhya Pradesh turn out to be from Kerala? Udayan, Jyotsna and I had a good laugh after spending the first few minutes conversing in Hindi. This was again the beauty of the unity in diversity of our country.

I saw children, some not even teenagers, out walking in groups well before sunrise. All through the route, whether in West Bengal, Jharkhand, Madhya Pradesh, Uttar Pradesh or Rajasthan, I saw the young training to get into the armed forces or the police force. They tested their bodies through sprints, long-distance runs, push-ups and other core exercises with visible determination and dedication. Boys and girls trained in groups, often with no coach. Many times, one of the fitter ones or the more enterprising ones took on the role of the mentor and led the sessions. I stopped every time and struck up a conversation; I found synergy in the fire that drove them. In army cantonments, I found myself running alongside small groups training for different internal contests and events. Tekanpur, near Gwalior, held one such lovely encounter.

I usually took a break after three hours had passed. On days that I was both walking and running, I completed between 19 and 21 km. On days I was only walking, I would be close to covering 17 km as

I took this break. I chose a spot that would rejuvenate me—a grove, a pretty mud house, a tea shop where a conversation with people was possible, a dhaba or even beneath a tree—as I still had another 10–15 km left to cover. These became my pit stops. I would settle down on my mat with my roller, after the use of which I would do some stretches and then have my sandwich, accompanied by a boiled egg at times. I also used a golf ball and a hockey ball to massage my foot and calf muscles, as advised by Sukdeb from HPC. I usually chose to change my shoes at this point and was on my way once again in about 15–30 minutes. Getting back into rhythm after the breakfast break took a little while, and I was certainly slower during the next couple of hours. The heat also slowed me down.

Oh yes! I did spend my time on phone calls while walking too. I shared my joys and angst with my husband while he walked wherever he was. My mother called me every day to check on me and hear from me. I video-called my children and my mother-in-law to show them the regions I was walking through. Rasya, who was managing this campaign on the back-end, called me every day between 9.15 a.m. and 10.30 a.m. and we spoke for an hour, planning upcoming interactions, discussing what would work on the presentations and what changes were needed, the route and the timeline. I must admit with regret that there were times and days when Rasya had to bear the brunt of my mood, which soured as the temperatures soared, and also as I reached the end of the day's journey in exhaustion. But she knew that I would be able to walk a couple of kilometres more if she kept me and my mind busy and played along. I can easily dedicate 200–300 km of my walk to my conversations with Rasya. Anushree, also from the team, would call to brief me on the places I was to pass through, informing me of their history, geography, flora, fauna and the people who made these places.

As I completed my mileage for the day, there was usually a flurry of activity. I drank my prescribed quantity of protein supplement during the last 30 minutes and scouted for a place to stretch. This spot often chose me rather than the other way around, which was usually close to wherever an interaction had been planned for that day—the premises of an NGO, a healthcare centre, the banks of a river, a school, a forecourt of a monument or a temple. On other days, I zeroed in on a shaded and pretty spot. There were occasions when such spots were hard to come by and I would end up doing my stretches on the mat by laying it out on the edge of the road next to the car. I was often surrounded by people who were intrigued and I was sometimes even asked if I was going to perform an acrobatic show for them.

After the stretches and the interaction as per the plan, I would hop into the car and get to my accommodation. We tried to organize a meal in advance as I was usually hit by desperate pangs of hunger as soon as I finished. I would eat with the team, then bathe and soak my feet in ice or cold water or use frozen gel packs as a cold compress. The logistics of ensuring that I had some ice or cold compress was quite a nightmare, and it did not work out in many places. I would then wear my compression stockings and lie on my back, my legs elevated for at least an hour. I considered myself fortunate when I managed to sleep. The adrenalin rush did not often allow sleep to take over. During the first month of the walk, this period of recovery was hard and painful; it was only after around 6 p.m. that I could walk without pain again when it was already time to prepare for the next day. The loneliness did not make this period any easier. But as days passed, I found that I felt rejuvenated after an hour of rest and the loneliness became a precious space in which I basked to reflect and ponder. I practised Yog Nidra on some days to strengthen my resolve and also to calm myself on days that were hard—and believe me, there *were* hard days. I left voice notes to myself and the team about my quest and my revelations.

Dinner was at 7.30 p.m. and I usually ate alone in my room. I spoke to the cook or the restaurant/kitchen myself to see what they could rustle up. It was two rotis, some plain rice, a bowl of yellow dal and a dry vegetable, whenever I could have my way. When walking by the vegetable markets, I noticed the vegetables that were available and negotiated with the annadatas (gods of food), the kitchen staff in this case, accordingly. Sometimes I succeeded, but very often I had to compromise and eat paneer (cottage cheese) or potatoes. By the end of the trip, I vowed that I would not eat paneer, potatoes, bread or peanut butter for a while; I had had so much of it. On one occasion, when we were lodged in the forest guest house in Betla, I had been served potatoes and dal for three meals already and I was aghast when I was promised the same fare for the fourth as well. The forest ranger visited me later that evening. He was kind enough to arrange for a night safari in the Betla forest and also instructed that I be served broccoli the next day for lunch. I was delighted by this variation, even if the broccoli was cooked in the same gravy as the potatoes!

I attempted to turn off the lights by 8.30 p.m. so that I could fall asleep by 9 p.m. and wake up fresh the next day. But there were many days when I had restless nights for different reasons.

I always woke up raring to go the next morning though. There was no typical day, only atypical days.

Walk,
and you shall know.
Walk,
and you shall grow.
Walk,
and walk alone.
Walk,
and walk together.
Walk,
and you shall be!

CHAPTER 24

I HAVE COMPANY

I had different types of companions on this journey, those who added meaning to my quest and those who gave me sleepless nights. I looked forward with anticipation when it came to the former, while I tackled the latter with bravado.

Curious co-travellers were always welcome and were often sources of information and insights into the history and the present of the land around us. They analysed the route and gave me tips about what I should not miss out on. Sometimes, policemen walked with me and were a huge help in connecting with personalities such as Sunita Devi, the rani mistry. I was pleasantly surprised and grateful that they had understood the reason for this walk well enough to be able to suggest appropriate interactions. They even helped us get permissions and access places that may have proved difficult to cross otherwise. I often challenged bystanders greeting me to walk some distance with me and was delighted when some did. We would chat as if we had known each other for ages on these walks. There would be questions about me, my family, my income, how I raised money for the trip, how the place I lived in was different from where they lived and much more. They were unabashed about satiating their curiosity and I had no reservations while answering them. After all, I was curious about their lives too and this had to be an equal relationship.

There were people who even solicited business partnerships, either directly with me or requested my help to reach others who might be interested. There were those aspiring to enlist in the police force or the army who thought I had the clout to get them responses to their applications. And then there were youngsters who were frank about wanting to work with me and asked where they could send their resumes. There were women who expressed their concern for me as a lone traveller and wanted to know how my family had supported me. In fact, there were times that my family and my husband were lauded in absentia more than I was.

Sports enthusiasts and runners were most eager to give me company. Davinder Singh and Umang from National Thermal Power Corporation would have happily run the whole distance instead of the 10 km they completed on the 29th day in Singrauli if duty had not called. Davinder had run a half marathon while Umang had completed a 10 km race, and both of them were in good shape. I was impressed to learn that Singrauli had hosted these races and that there had been a good number of participants. Anjali, the Head of the Department of Architecture at Madhav Institute of Technology and Science (MITS), Gwalior, and her husband, Sanjay, are both cycling enthusiasts and rode close to 20 km to catch up and welcome me on the outskirts of Gwalior. They dream of a cross-country cycling trip and I am sure they will realize it someday. Students and faculty of different colleges of architecture and representatives from different chapters of the IIA also brightened different days of my walk with their presence.

If I saw a group of women, children or even construction workers walking ahead of me, I quickened my pace to walk a few steps with them. Sometimes, if they were behind me, they would do the same to catch up to know more about this woman who did not fit in. This brought me a fair share of friends. Mithu, a health worker in Champadanga, told me about her chosen vocation and the challenges she had faced. She recounted how the community had rallied together to keep everyone safe during COVID and was satisfied that there were no major incidents in her locality. Ram Lakhan from Khajuri in Madhya Pradesh is a construction worker in the city and he turns into a contractor once he comes back to his village and brings with him his expertise and sense of aesthetics and design.

My husband, Bala, joined me on the 34th day at Rewa, which also happened to be Holi. I was fortunate to have a constant companion for a while, and he walked around 400 km of the 1700 with me for the next two weeks. Until now, we had connected on phone calls, when he would walk in Kolkata and I would walk wherever I was. These morning calls were spent describing to him the details of what I was seeing, feeling and learning. We had serious discussions on issues that

I was observing, which I hoped would guide the future of the Ethos Foundation. Now that he was walking with me, Bala experienced first-hand the jaunt through Madhya Pradesh. He left me to myself on the 51st day at Dabra. The 400 km that we walked together strengthened what we shared. He completely understood that this was my 1700 and allowed me to set the pace. There was no moment where he put himself or his needs before mine. There was no expert advice to make me change anything that I was doing. He did not feel left out when I stole the limelight during interactions and gently stepped out of the way when photographs and videos were being taken for documentation. I bid him farewell knowing he would be there with me as I crossed over into Delhi.

There were others too, the kinds whose company I did not relish. I mentioned earlier that I felt like Pied Piper with curious children following me. But I had mice keeping me company too, and I am certainly not a big fan of mice.

To convey how paranoid I am, I'll relate an incident from my past. Bala and I had just gotten married. I had reached home early and decided to rustle up a quick meal before Bala reached so that we could spend the rest of the time we had together. As I got the box of rice out of the cupboard, a mouse jumped out and whizzed past me. I was in a state of utter panic and locked myself on the balcony for the next couple of hours until Bala got home. The feeling of a mouse crawling on my leg kept me and Bala up the whole night. Surely I have come a long way since then and do not react in such an extreme manner, but I cannot live with mice in the same room.

But mice actually chose to keep me company at different locations. As I was stretching outside a cement shop whose shutters were down, I saw a couple of them playing peek-a-boo. Did I run for cover? No, I just lay there looking at them and calmly completed my stretches. It happened again when we had just checked into our rooms in a small motel. I had unpacked, bathed and was just getting ready to rest for a bit when I noticed some flashes of movement in the room. I first thought my eyes were playing games with me until I spotted it happily scampering across the bed. I kicked up a fuss with the hotel manager, and they changed my room and moved all my things. I then went through the exercise of unpacking and packing my bag again, just in case the mouse had travelled with me to the newly allotted room. Then there was the time when the room of the lodge we were staying in had a false ceiling. Just as I turned off my lights at night to sleep, the mice began to play. And this was no ordinary party! I would have believed it if someone had told me that these were monkeys on a tin roof. That was the kind of ruckus they were creating, and with their squeaks, it turned into quite an orchestra. I had to draw on immense fortitude to get through such nights. I covered myself by pulling the blanket over my head, and used philosophy to curb my dread. 'Fear does not exist anywhere but in the mind' said Dale Carnegie, and I tried to believe it. I attempted to inhale courage and exhale my fear. The first time was tough but gradually, I learned the art of keeping such fears at bay and was able to sleep in peace for the few hours that I had before the alarm woke me up. I learnt to deal with other creepy crawlies too.

But these were not the only pests that I encountered.

I faced a difficult night the day we reached Mauranipur. I chose to have an early dinner and went to bed. I woke up to running, thumping, dancing and a lot of chatter right outside my door. Bollywood numbers were being belted loud enough for the whole of Mauranipur to enjoy and the cacophony only got worse as the night wore on. My heart seemed to be thumping to the beat.

We learnt that the noise was coming from a birthday party, and it only got more unruly and boisterous, making me concerned. We have heard enough stories of how some of these parties end. I was tempted to wake my team up and suggest that we begin walking at night to the next destination. At around 2 a.m. things got quieter, and I got an hour's rest before I rose to walk again.

Emotions of different kinds kept me company too: joy and exhilaration, pain and resolve, awe and appreciation, confusion and calm, anxiety and anger.

Alone, and with company, this was my journey to complete!

CHAPTER 25

ALMOST THERE! OH, WAIT!

Day 54
7 April 2022

While 90 per cent of the distance has been covered; 50 per cent of the journey is still left! I reached Gwalior dancing down its hilly terrain. We had requested a young photographer with a drone to accompany us as we neared Gwalior, and he was impressed by my stamina. I had slipped into my groove and was cruising along nicely. Just the evening before, I had walked an additional 10 km after a long and hard day, making a total of 36 km—the second-highest distance to be covered in a day by me on this trip. I had 311 km left of the 1700. I felt good.

7 April was to be a rest day. I had accepted an invitation from an enthusiastic group of cyclists to interact with them. The 'I Love Gwalior' selfie point was where we all met and made some memories. Then I was offered a cycle to ride with them. I accepted their offer and got on the cycle and our group of around twenty set off.

I am not an expert cyclist. I have cycled only for entertainment, at best to get from one place to another in the past. It had been at least a decade since I had gotten on a cycle and here I was, cycling with professional cyclists. I was to cycle only a couple of kilometres but soon realized that the park where we were to meet and interact was over 5 km away. I decided to get off and walk the rest of the distance as I was becoming increasingly uncomfortable. Only Shantanu and Param from our team joined us to document the interaction. They were ahead of me on a motorcycle, taking pictures and videos.

And then it happened! I braked, not so gently, swung my leg off the seat and found out that my leg would not reach the ground! The cycle was too high. I came crashing to the ground, the cycle atop me, and my cyclist friends and team watched in horror. Param later recollected that he had been sure that my head had struck a stone. I remember someone moving the cycle and helping me to my feet. There were minor bruises on my palms as I had used them to break my fall. As I walked, I felt a sharp pain in my left foot. I got on a motorcycle and reached the park, where I took off my shoes to see a shiny bump on my foot. My heart sank. This was not happening!

I kept my cool and chatted with all those gathered as I iced my foot in the hope that the swelling would magically disappear. In about half an hour, I confronted the reality that I needed medical attention. We zeroed in on a couple of doctors to consult and reached the nursing home. Vinayak too had reached the nursing home in the car. One look at my foot, and the doctor said, 'It looks like your journey is over.'

He was sure it was a fracture or a bad ligament injury. I was advised an X-ray to ascertain the severity.

Anjali, my friend, architect and cyclist, through whom this interaction had been fixed, was miserable. She suggested that we should consult another doctor and then off we went to Dr Pukhraj Gaur. He had specialized in rehabilitation medicine and was a part of the cycling group. However, Dr Gaur's verdict was similar to the previous doctor's. As it was still early morning, the X-ray technician had not yet arrived and so, the doctor conducted the X-ray himself. I heaved a sigh of relief when he said that it was not a fracture but a trauma injury. I would need time to heal. He was not willing to hazard a guess on how long it would take to heal just yet. Besides painkillers and anti-inflammatory medicines, the advice was to rest as much as possible, use an ice pack on the area every hour for around 10 minutes, use an ankle binder and keep my leg elevated. RICE—rest, ice, compress and elevate—is the first-level medical advice for such injuries. He recounted a time when he had been similarly injured while attending a conference and these measures had helped him heal enough to be able to drive back in 24 hours. But he said it would take me a minimum of a week to 10 days to be able to walk again. He would not comment on whether I would be able to take the rigour of the rest of the journey yet.

I returned to my hotel a little crushed. The back-end team was informed and gloom descended on the whole team. We decided not to share this information on social media yet. We were meant to take three rest days in Gwalior, and I was anyway ahead of schedule. I slept the rest of the morning away and woke up wondering if it had all been a bad dream. Feeling the pain in my foot, the soreness all over my body and the swelling, I knew I was in a spot. I called my husband and allowed myself a good cry.

But after that call, I underwent a magical transformation; I felt a wave of peace sweeping over me, and the words 'the journey is the destination' floated into my conscience. Despite the predicament I was in, I felt no alarm.

I almost felt good.

The IIA Madhya Pradesh Chapter had arranged a little gathering of the local architects of Gwalior the next evening and I chose to continue with my agenda. I am glad I did. Meeting new people and being with friends elevated my spirits and helped my team as well, even though I felt their pitiful eyes on me as I limped across the room. This was where I met Dr Alok Sharma, the director of IITTM (Indian Institute of Tourism and Travel Management), Gwalior, and Ramakrishna Kongalla, an authority in Indian iconography and a professor. I already realized the value Dr Sharma brought to the discipline of travel and tourism with his training as an architect. I immediately struck up a conversation, and it resulted in a session being held with students of IITTM the next day. There were students from different parts of India who had many intelligent observations and questions, which led to a fertile discussion on collaboration between the fields of architecture and tourism to strengthen them both. Eventually, we had to break the session as it was well past their lunch break and their next class was to commence. I was gifted a terracotta sculpture created by Sri Mukund Ketkar, a renowned sculptor from Gwalior.

The painkillers were helping. I was able to walk, not with much pain, but I knew I had to follow the doctor's orders like they were gospel. I was also in touch with Dr Sanjay Chatterjee in Kolkata, keeping him informed of the developments. I rested as much as I could, but I also used this time for brief outings to meet people and learn more about Gwalior. I ran a virtual office and an opportunity to meet an employee was not to be missed. Radhika was a young student of architecture at MITS, Gwalior, and an intern with us. I am glad that we made time to meet at least a few times during my stay in Gwalior and she arranged for me to meet women from a local community through the NGO, Ekal Yuva.

Showstopper 27

During my visit to MITS, I made the acquaintance of Gayatri Singh, the director of Jai Vilas Palace Museum, who is grace personified. My earlier itinerary did not leave me with much time for a leisurely visit to the palace, but I now had all the time in the world. I tied up with her for a tour of the palace, conducted by Avni, the archivist. Avni gave us an overview of the 41 galleries of the palace and took me through the Durbar Hall. A 'Photo Angrakha' caught my eye—there were photographs of the king and his parents printed on the fabric, that was then fashioned into an outfit! Gayatri explained that pagri or turban-tying was a craft, undertaken with great passion, and she spoke of her intent to nurture a woman Pagadbandh (a skilled turban artist) into the male-dominated profession.

Gayatri walked me through the forecourt, which boasted of a crystal fountain, and pointed to where the descendant from the royal family, Jyotiraditya Scindia, received greetings from his staff. The Lalitpur Gate was exclusively reserved for the royal family. The highlight of this visit was the dining hall on the first floor with its three huge dining tables that could seat fifty people each. One of the staff members proudly showed me a silver train that weighed 24 kg. The miniature gadget ran on a track around the table and carried decanters that held wine and cigars. These decanter slots were also brakes, and every time a decanter was lifted by someone to help themselves, the train stopped, and after the decanter had been replaced, it resumed its journey. The kings had indeed been fond of toys and gizmos. This contraption is in fine fettle and the dining room is still used for special occasions. I was also enthralled at how the temperature in the palace had been regulated despite there being no artificial means of heating or cooling. The 8-foot-wide walls and the high ceilings played their role well. My date with the Jai Vilas Palace ended with a delightful chat with the team that worked on curating exhibits, guiding people and maintaining the palace.

I visited Dr Gaur every day and would look at him with puppy eyes, hoping that he would allow me to walk. The inflammation had definitely reduced, but the pain persisted. He said that under normal circumstances, he would have certainly advised complete rest for two weeks. But these were not normal circumstances. On the morning of the sixth day, he allowed me to try walking the road again. He was clear that I was not to walk more than 5 km the first time. I was then to wait for a few hours and then walk a few more kilometres, given that the pain and the swelling did not worsen. I set off in the blistering afternoon sun at 1 p.m. for a 5 km saunter and rested up until 5 p.m. when I followed up with an 8-kilometre walk. With baby steps, I was back on my feet, and soon out of Gwalior the next day.

I took care to not walk more than 20 km a day for the next week. The painkillers were helping—I was completely pain-free and used k-tape to minimize stress on the ankle. Whenever I came upon undulating surfaces, my foot reminded me of the fall. Dr Gaur certainly helped. While we wished to tag him on Instagram and thank him for his help, the simple man did not know much about social media! He did not charge for treating me as he had resonated with my journey. Every so often on the 1700, I realized that this world is full of good people. We allow a minority of bad episodes to colour our understanding of this world.

I replayed the moment of my fall often in the few days that followed, imagining the different decisions I could have made resulting in different outcomes. I could have actually been injured far worse, and the 1700 may not have mattered any more. I could have been firm about not getting on the bicycle and could have met the cyclists at the park directly. I would then have stuck to my schedule and not learnt a valuable lesson on the importance of single-minded focus and concentration. I would have missed out on all the other lovely people I was able to make time for.

As the saying goes, all is well that ends well.

Walk,
for joy.
Walk,
for peace.
Walk,
to love.
Walk,
to be loved.
Walk,
and you shall heal.

CHAPTER 26

YOUR BODY IS YOUR TEMPLE

Ankon Mitra, my young architect friend residing in Delhi, is the co-author of my first book, *Archumen: Questioning Architecture.*[26] When I called to wish him for his birthday from Gwalior, he expressed wonderment at my awe-inspiring adventure and joked that he would touch my feet in respect when he met me next. And I replied in jest at that point, saying that I needed to touch my own feet too. But the more I reflected on these words, the more I felt a deep sense of love for my body. It had cooperated with me to its fullest. The extreme stress I placed on my body—the aches, the throbbing pain at night—made me value every part of it for playing along through this fulfilling journey. My feet and lower limbs were being put through a great deal of rigour every day, and were coping well. I would not say that there were no signs of wear and tear. The hot metallic surface of the road caused constant pain in the balls of my feet, and it made its presence felt even when I was not walking. This pain took a while, much after the 1700, to completely go away.

While in humid West Bengal and Jharkhand, I started using an absorbent powder on my feet, which I would layer inside my socks to keep them dry. This was also to arrest any fungal infection due to perspiration. Not comprehending the impact, I did not discontinue this practice as I entered Uttar Pradesh and Madhya Pradesh where the weather gradually got drier. A few days into this region, I started feeling a tenderness in the soles of my feet and attributed this to the effect of the hot surface, little realizing that I needed to do the reverse of what I had been doing so far—moisturize more and stop using the powder. The skin on the soles of my feet started to peel

[26]Balakrishnan, Gita, and Ankon Mitra, *Archumen: Questioning Architecture*, Ethos, Kolkata, 1 January 2014.

and my feet were hurting a lot more. When they seemed on their way to becoming very sensitive, I called our family physician in Kolkata, Dr Sandeep Sangar, who suggested that I discontinue the powder and prescribed a simple moisturizing cream. This made a world of difference in a few days.

Listen to your body and you will be much better off. There are telltale signs every day from our body, telling us what it likes and does not like through reactions to different external and internal stimuli. Allergies, extreme weight gain or weight loss, body aches, ulcers and hair loss are all communication mechanisms of the body, telling us that we are not doing something right and that lifestyle changes may be necessary. Even in cases where the body responds to an internal stimulus, as when there is an underlying disease, our body is crying for us to seek medical help. Being aware of different sensations and our reactions will help us connect better with our bodies.

I was at the office of the commissioner of police, Faridabad, interacting with a group of high-performing cops in their conference room. Now when I see the photographs and the footage of this interaction, I am quite struck by my conversation on fitness. I was speaking with folks who are in a profession of making places safe for us, and can do so because of their fitness! At some point during the interaction, there was curiosity about my age from the male policemen and the women officers wanted to know about my diet and the cosmetics I used to maintain my skin. When I revealed to them that I was nearing fifty-four, they gasped in disbelief. I pulled off my bandanna so that my greys would make it believable for them. They laughed and retorted that people streak their hair to sport a salt-and-pepper chic look these days. These questions were common at various interactions, including one with a hard-working youth group of the Federation of Rajasthan Trade and Industry (FORTI), Bharatpur.

I had never given any thought to how my skin would react to the exposure to pollution, wind and sun. Keeping my diet simple and drinking plenty of water must have played a key role. Eating light was awfully tough as we had no control over what we would be served on any day. I did carry some sunscreen with me, but I gave up using it within a few days because it meant carrying it on me and remembering to use it when the sun got harsh. I did find my exposed skin getting angry at times, but I gradually acclimated to the changes. So besides simple moisturisers, I was using nothing for protection. I definitely came out of the 1700 a lot browner and darker. The tan lines lasted over many weeks, helping me cherish the memories a lot longer.

The body, mind and soul need to be adequately nourished for a journey of this kind to be accomplished and for it to be meaningful. My mind played a crucial role on the 1700 as it had to keep me motivated and charged to live every moment of the day, however exhausted my physical self was. There were times when doubts crept in: will my body survive this extreme regime I was putting it through? I realized I had to keep my mind busy to keep such thoughts at bay. I found great solace in connecting with people. Hearing of their struggles and discovering their indomitable spirits made my pain paltry and temporary. I read quite a bit but found it hard to concentrate when I was tired. Also, the lighting systems within most of our accommodations did not make indoor reading easy on the eyes. I spent a lot of time sitting and staring into the vast open, meditating on what 'is'. I also started developing a blueprint for the future, after the 1700, in my mind. As I engaged with communities, I examined with excitement the possibilities of these interactions leading to a project. I closely visualized how these different projects would be executed. I evaluated the duration and the costs of these endeavours and thought of ways to raise funds. I discussed all this with my back-end team so they could begin their homework and we could get to work as soon as I concluded the 1700.

All this was nourishment for my soul. The gamut of possibilities awaiting me beyond the 1700 was probably one of the reasons for my perseverance even when I was down and out and came upon some really hard days.

CHAPTER 27

KHAMMA GANI

Day 59 to Day 60
12 April 2022 to 13 April 2022

'*Padharo mhare des* (welcome to our land)' may not have actually been on every inhabitant's lips as I had witnessed in the more touristy Jaipur, Udaipur, Jaisalmer and Jodhpur in the past, but the emotion was palpable at every moment of my short walk through Rajasthan. We had left the highways behind. I walked past quaint hamlets and through huge farmlands blissfully. Men in colourful, large turbans and women in bright sarees and skirts always seemed to have time for us, for a cup of tea or a snack, to give us directions or to just chat. Camels as a mode of transportation became a common sight.

Even before I entered Rajasthan on foot, the Rajasthan Chapter of the IIA—Ar. Gaurav Agarwal, Ar. Mukul Goyal, Ar. Rekha Nemani and Anu Sogani from Save our City, an NGO—had organized an insightful interaction off the route with residents at Bharatpur—a women's group, who interestingly called themselves the 'Mom's Club', FORTI, FORTI Youth Wing and some people in local governance were a part of this interaction. Having been to Bharatpur in the past, I had already ticked off the sights on a tourist's list. I instead chose to visit Shri Bihari Ji temple.

Dholpur used to be a part of Bharatpur district but was made into a separate district in 1982. Dholpur is an important site for architects; a type of sandstone used in different parts of India is quarried in this district and sourced here. This pinkish-red sandstone is what we see at the Agra Fort, which is only 56 km from Dholpur. This region, like most of Rajasthan, is rich in craftspeople who work with stone. Even the common folk understand the material and are able to handle simple construction themselves. However, it appears that there is now a trend to veer away from actual stone construction towards brick or the more recent concrete blocks and cloak it in plaster.

The impression that homes made of brick and plaster (or those that look like they are) are more prosperous, reared its head once again. I saw homes made from the beautiful Dholpur stone being plastered as well. The locals explained that this helped elevate their prestige in society, and was even an important factor in finding brides or grooms from well-to-do families for their children. They, however, already knew that they were increasing the cost of their homes and that of recurring maintenance.

This public perception needs to change and the glory of local identity needs to be restored. Jerusalem is a city of stone too, and all you can see around you is white limestone or dolomite—so much so that this stone has come to be known as Jerusalem Stone. A place gets its character from its natural resources, its architecture and its people, and all need to be in harmony for a distinct regional identity to flourish. Architecture, after all, should belong to the place and its people.

On a subsequent visit to Jaipur, I met Varun Sharma of Aravali, an NGO based in Jaipur working with multiple organizations to support marginalized communities across Rajasthan. He told me of the tragedy of stonecutters and their vulnerability to silicosis, a disease caused by inhaling stone dust. The dust they breathe in reaches their lungs, and over time, their lymph nodes begin to calcify, making respiration difficult. Varun spoke of a village called Bugdar in the Karauli district of Rajasthan with the highest number of silicosis widows—as their spouses have passed away due to silicosis. As architects extensively rely on stone as a material, they should also be vocal about responsible quarrying and stonecutting practices.

In earlier periods of history, chhatris or pavilions were made out of stone as a mark of respect for famous people who had passed away, and were also symbols of victory in battle. Many such chhatris dotted my path, but the more recently built ones had been constructed with brick and concrete.

The proportions of these chhatris made them an attractive sight and they were inviting to an exhausted traveller on a hot day. A quick pause, the cat's pose of yoga or even a short snooze, and I was ready to conquer some more miles!

Showstopper 28

The most unforgettable face during this part of the journey was Jashoda's. To me she appeared to be over nine decades old, but she claimed, with her eyes twinkling, that she was around seventy. She was returning from the fields when we met and she was kindness personified. While her body was small and frail, her zest for life was infectious. She lived with her grandson and his family. She was liberal in thought and encouraged her great-granddaughter to pursue higher studies, even though her father was a farmer. She was the matriarch of the community around her and was hugely respected. While she nostalgically recalled time with her husband, one of the finest stone carvers of this region, she was completely at peace with her present life.

The warmth of her hug brings happiness to me even now, on a tough day. She recited Kabir's couplet for me, which goes: 'Mann ke haare haar hai, mann ke jeete jeet. Kahe Kabir Hari paiye, mann hi ki parteet.' This speaks of the power of the mind that can define the difference between failure and success.

CHAPTER 28

UNITY IN BIODIVERSITY

Peacocks dancing upon my path; nilgai, hares and deer crossing over; sections full of weaver birds; the mahua tree (important for many communities); the racket of birds in Chhatarpur in Madhya Pradesh; the safaris in Panna and Betla national parks—they told a story of India's rich biodiversity.

Morena, 46 km from Gwalior, gets its name from 'mor', meaning peacock, and justifiably so. Morena accounts for the highest number of peacocks in India. Some say that the Mauryan Empire got its name from this majestic bird. Peacocks were a common sight all the way from Morena to Mathura, sitting atop trees, making low gentle flights, calling out to each other, and sometimes coquettishly displaying their brilliant, open plumage in the middle of the road. We once even heard its high-pitched honk and were left wondering what had irked the bird. Peacocks prey on snakes, and it probably meant that there were snakes in this region too. As if to corroborate this assumption, we found people not using the wilderness as toilets but using places closer to their homes—probably due to the fear of snakes. There were a couple of occasions on dark mornings when the rustling sounds from the vegetation near me had me wondering if a snake was slithering by.

I did come across a few snakes lying dead on the road, all curled up. I was enlightened by Sonam, a valuable member of our Ethos team, that snakes are cold-blooded creatures and come onto the tarred roads at night seeking warmer temperatures. They are also sluggish in their movement compared to other fast-moving animals. Consequently, they are sometimes crushed by moving traffic.

In cities, dogs and cats are largely domesticated, and those that belong to no one scavenge or depend on the passers-by and their goodwill for survival. In villages, it seemed as if all dogs belonged to everyone and no one in particular. There was one calf I came upon that behaved not very differently from a puppy, prancing around naughtily while urging all the children around to play with her. I chanced upon a particularly fascinating conversation between a goatherd and her family of goats. She was herding them with a whistling sound—but not quite a whistle—and they were responding to her call by making sounds and following the route she wanted them to take. The sounds the goats made were very different from the bleats that I was accustomed to.

To initiate conversations with little children, I carried a presentation with me, titled 'Learning from Nature', and it showed videos of how bees made their hives, ants made anthills and the weaver birds made their nests. Almost all the children had seen a weaver bird's nest but not how the nest was made, and this excited them. I could relate to their excitement when we walked through an area between Kheragarh in Uttar Pradesh and Dholpur in Rajasthan and saw hundreds of weaver bird nests dangling from trees. This was the baya weaver bird, the most common of the four varieties and the only one found in India.

On another occasion, the birds made sure to keep everyone wide awake in the wee hours of the morning at Chhatarpur. There were hundreds of them. It seemed that they were offering morning salutations to each other simultaneously, over and over. It was utterly cacophonic and fascinating. I got wiser after a chat with a nature enthusiast. This region is a roosting site for parrots and they flock to their roosts as the day ends and wake up chirping together as they begin their day. I had reached their roosting site as they were starting their day and was fortunate to have been a part of their morning. Parrots usually roost on sheesham (*Dalbergia sissoo*), babul (*Acacia arabica*) and semal (*Salmalia malabarica*), which are found in abundance in the Bundelkhand region.

The tree cover and their variety changed from state to state, and within states too. I felt nostalgic when I came across trees I had seen before in Hyderabad as a child. I walked through the alluvial soil of West Bengal, where the general climate is tropical and humid with heavy rainfall in many parts; this helps provide a high green cover. The state tree of West Bengal is the blackboard tree, locally known as 'chhatim' or 'saptaparni', a pretty tree with bunches of white flowers. As I moved into Jharkhand, the landscape turned hilly and the soil was largely laterite. Although the sal tree was plentiful in West Bengal too, it rightfully has the privilege of being Jharkhand's state tree. Fruit-bearing trees like the mango and the bael trees were abundant, and it was interesting to see the flowering patterns on the trees, the side facing the sun bearing maximum flowers. The colours of the leaves varied through a single tree, dependent on the exposure to sunlight. On this trip, I learnt that every state has a state tree and I tried to spot the dignified banyan tree in Madhya Pradesh, the sublime ashoka in Uttar Pradesh, the hardy khejri in Rajasthan and the peepal in Haryana.

Showstopper 29

The mahua tree and its role in the lives of villagers, particularly the tribal community, was an important discovery during the 1700. Mahua or *Madhuca longifolia* is a native tropical tree that is considered sacred. It finds mention in the ancient treatise on healthcare, *Charaka Samhita*, as well as in the *Atharva Veda*. Different parts of the tree are used for treating various diseases, such as worms, respiratory infections, diabetes, dental problems, rheumatism, eczema and much more. The ash from the burned leaves is used as a poultice to treat burns and other injuries. The fruit has a high nutritional value. As the saying goes, 'A bite of the mahua and you will not know hunger.' During the famines of 1770 and 1896–97, the seed cakes from the mahua tree became the staple diet for the poor. Also known as the Indian butter tree, its flowers are distilled into the most original native home-brewed liquor through a process that lasts eight days.

The sweet smell of the mahua flowers often reached my nostrils before my eyes could spot the tree; the carpet of green flowers under it was being combed through by women, children and sometimes even men. Christened the 'tree of life', the mahua has been a tree of survival during times of scarcity and during the pandemic too.

Walking and running through the thick forest cover on the roads of Panna was uplifting. Seeing a barking deer, a wild dog, hares and squirrels on the road made my heart skip a beat every time. When discussing the risk of setting out before sunrise in Panna, I was reassured that there was no concern at all and that, at most, I might run into a sloth bear which would leave seeing the headlights I donned. That was not particularly reassuring, but I was happy to not cross paths with a sloth bear. However, seeing a sloth bear running with her baby on her back was a sight to behold on the safari at Panna Forest Reserve on our rest day! Having been rather unlucky at spotting the most sought-after sights on most of our past safaris, seeing a leopard walk gently, pose for us and slowly cross our path made for a very fulfilling rest day.

We were fortunate to have been able to secure accommodation at the forest guest house at Betla National Park in Jharkhand, and I discovered that it was designed by Sandeep Jha, an architect and friend from Ranchi. The night safari, offered by the forest ranger, made for a quiet drive through the jungles at night, spotting chitals, sambhars, langurs, monkeys and giant squirrels.

The monkeys in Betla were extremely naughty. They were everywhere as the sun came out, and I had to seek the help of the caretakers to get into my room on the first floor and escape them. They were adept at opening the sliding door and entering rooms through the balcony and would even knock at the door like a human. One had to have all their wits around to outwit them. But when we returned from the safari at night, they were asleep, not quite like babies, but almost. This was the first time I saw monkeys sleeping while sitting on a narrow ledge, clinging to each other. They looked so innocent—unlike the bullies they were in the daytime. As I entered my room at night, I was welcomed by a display of lights; some fireflies had found their way into my room!

Unity in biodiversity! I borrowed the title for this chapter from a recent hoarding the forest department put up but the term 'biodiversity' is said to have been coined by Walter G. Rosen in 1985, while its protracted form, 'biological diversity' was first used in 1916 by J. Arthur Harris and simply refers to the variety and variability of life on earth; the term started being used in India after 2012.

What can better express the need for the convergence of ideas, people and systems to protect our ecosystem? 'Unity in Biodiversity' beautifully conveys the balance that must be maintained for our universe to survive and thrive.

CHAPTER 29

HISTORY'S TRAILS AND
INVISIBLE MONUMENTS

A journey through any part of India on foot, by car or even by train is akin to travelling through a living exhibition of art, culture, craft, music and architecture, spanning different periods in time. Of these, architecture and building are a combined expression of different skills coming together to display narratives of lives and lifestyles. Archaeologists go to great lengths, or in this case depths, to excavate the ruins of buildings to unravel the mysteries of ancient times gone by. Historic buildings are windows that give you a glimpse into what was. They can be time machines to travel to an era that we never were a part of.

As I walked the 1700, I often felt that I was walking back and forth across time, crossing buildings and structures dating back to different periods. Bishnupur, Daltonganj, Alipura, Nagod, Wyndhamganj, Jhansi, Orchha, Gwalior and Datia were some of the larger towns and cities with resplendent heritage. The façade of the religious monuments changed in appearance as I moved from the terracotta temples of Bishnupur, with their char-chala and at-chala roofs (four-way and eight-way sloping roofs), to more curvilinear shikharas in temples of Jharkhand and Uttar Pradesh. Domed roofs made their appearance even in religious structures in Madhya Pradesh. Forts dotted the landscape all through, giving the towns of Datia, Daltonganj, Gwalior, Jhansi, Orchha and Satna an aura of power and formidability.

Both the Baghelkhand and the Bundelkhand regions of Madhya Pradesh and Uttar Pradesh are rich with palaces, of which some are functional even today. The palace of Nagod told a story of how times had changed. The cost of its upkeep was proving a challenge for the scions currently residing there.

The descendants of the royal family at Alipura took a different route. They had converted their palace into a heritage tourism property to generate revenue for its maintenance. I had the opportunity of availing the hospitality of Rao Bahadur Raja Manvendra Singh Judeo at Alipura Palace. Most portions of the palace are 300-years-old and some parts are 150-years-old. I imagined a life unknown to me— walking up and down the steep stairs, exercising in the courtyard, eating in the dining chambers, watching the sunset from the terrace— steeped in luxury but fraught with uncertainties.

Showstopper 30

Harnarayan Rai is a mason who handles all the repair and restoration work at Alipura Palace. He opined that people were switching to using newer materials and methods of renovating old structures because older techniques were labour-intensive and far too expensive. He rued the fact that the know-how and skill to use such materials and tools is also waning. He has been involved in the upkeep of old buildings for over thirty years, following in the footsteps of his father who also worked in the same zilla. His father had been introduced to masonry by an expert mason visiting from Varanasi. He spoke of different experiments that he had been involved in, where the new met the old; thicker walls gave way to cavity walls; cavity walls where, at times, the cavity was filled with mud. Rai believes that more training programmes in these techniques should be available so the style can flourish and possibilities of employment can grow.

Through our conversations, he evoked in me a sense of nostalgia.

Showstopper 31

Ram Singh Yadav is a daily wage farmhand living in Alipura village with his wife and five children. His wife also works on nearby farms. Their occupation keeps them busy for four months or so a year, and the money they make has to last them the rest of the year.

They recently got financial assistance under the Pradhan Mantri Awas Yojana to renovate their home. Under this scheme, Yadav said, a family is entitled to ₹1,50,000, which is dispensed in four instalments. The first three instalments of ₹40,000 each are released in three stages on completion of the masonry work to the lintel level, while the balance, ₹30,000, is reimbursed as labour cost. An additional ₹12,000 is given towards the construction of a toilet. The government engineers inspect the site regularly.

Ram Singh Yadav agreed that this kind of upgradation of village homes is leading to a complete transformation of the countryside—visually as well as intangibly—through the ways in which the people interact. The verandas at the threshold of every home have now been sacrificed and consequently, the casual interactions held there, through which a sense of community had thrived, have also been lost.

Design guidelines integrated into such schemes should have a clear understanding of the local context. With the involvement of the people, these schemes can ensure the deliverance of an evolving but regional and local identity.

Showstopper 32

As I walked through Dhubela, I was introduced to the valour of Maharaja Chhatrasal, a mediaeval Indian warrior from the seventeenth century who took up his sword against the Mughal Emperor Aurangzeb and established his kingdom in Bundelkhand.

I had never heard of the cenotaph of Maharani Kamlapati, also known as Rani Devkunwari of Chhatrasal. A young girl, while minding her father's shop, drew my attention to it and told me that she and her brother visited this wonder often. On the Chhatarpur–Nowgong–Jhansi highway, this octagonal cenotaph is located on the banks of Dhubela River and is a double-storeyed structure with a domed roof. It is 16 km away from Chhatarpur and 64 km from Khajuraho and is a fine example of Bundeli architecture with latticed windows and a stunning ceiling. It has 180 paintings and frescoes on the walls and 48 petaled lotus flowers over its seven domes. It is a pity that this structure does not even have a Wikipedia page for itself, even though it is one of the few cenotaphs in India built for a queen.

Showstopper 33

We reached this beauty on a hot afternoon and the patterns of light and shadow on the interior floors and walls added to the drama of the story of this brave queen. We were informed that this structure was being restored by the state government and work was in progress. I climbed to the topmost level and saw the workmen perched on the scaffolding. One of the skilled craftsmen seemed happy to come down and he shared details of his passion for restoration with me.

Chintamani Vishwakarma, from the village of Newari in Madhya Pradesh, works as a contractor, mostly on restoration projects. While an engineer from the state's archaeological department oversaw the project and visited regularly to give them instructions and recipes for the lime mortar, etc., over time, Chintamani had grown to become adept and an expert in his own way. He has been associated with projects for the archaeological department for over twelve years now and has learnt his way through apprenticeships. Now those under him learn through the same 'guru-shishya parampara' (teacher–student relationship). He began his stint with a project in Ramraja Nagari in Orchha and he believes in the need to safeguard repositories of traditional wisdom.

While watching a sound-and-light show at the Orchha Fort and using guide services at many historical sites, I was reminded of the legends and myths we build around our buildings. Drama and storytelling play an important role in romanticizing little nooks, the stunning stone-inlay work and the peephole in a door. This mythicizing cannot be undermined as it breathes life into a structure that would otherwise be desolate and forgotten.

While our history textbooks—even those from the architecture college curriculum—mostly describe large temples, monuments and forts, the sights I saw along the way had me wistfully wishing that the real story of these relatively lesser-known monuments could also find their way into history classes. These innumerable smaller monuments, together with the large ones, make up the history of a place.

A monument is defined as a building or a structure of historical importance. Every time I walked past the vast and scattered monuments, several questions dogged me. These monuments were crafted and built by the fine hands of common people. Do we know enough about where they lived? Do we know of the places where they laid their loved ones to rest? Do we know where they learnt their craft, went to shop, to rest, to play at leisure? Do we know where they lay low for safety and security?

Architecture—the oldest art of civilization, of shelter-making, of putting a roof over one's head—must tell all stories equally. Only then we will be fully informed about what civilization during certain eras truly looked like. We know of the exquisite details of the sites where the kings and queens bathed; we know of the magnificent mausoleums and tombs where their kin were laid to rest; we know of the massive, impenetrable forts where the rajas lay low in the face of a siege. Monuments are important. Their construction nurtured talent and skills, enabled livelihoods and told stories of a certain time—albeit partially. Many monuments were built with this intention. Do those conceptualizing our monuments today even realize this need?

'A bicycle shed is a building; Lincoln Cathedral is a piece of architecture,' Nikolaus Pevsner wrote in his book,[27] but does this attitude lead to the neglect of buildings and spaces used every day by common people? The bling, glitz and glamour of monuments may have relevance to the ways of building and technologies for the privileged, but we have been learning, studying and documenting the lives and cultures only of certain elite societies. How much of what we learn from these large monuments can be applied to buildings of much smaller scale? From that viewpoint, do we not have so much more to learn from the homes of people? To me, these are our invisible monuments!

Showstopper 34

It was my lucky day. I was trudging wearily along my path when I was beckoned from across the road by Jagjiwan and Vidyapath, two

---

[27]Pevsner, Nikolaus, *An Outline of European Architecture (2nd edition)*, Thames and Hudson Ltd, High Holborn, London, 7 September 2009.

brothers from a small village named Bharra in Madhya Pradesh. I was tempted to just wave back and keep walking but I am so glad that they persisted and brought me to their home. The house was quite a gem. A little later, a small crowd had gathered to explain the story of the house in an animated manner.

This house was built in 1972 and hence is a piece of history, fifty years old. The family built this home, and Jagjiwan and Vidhyapath's father was the main designer. It was indeed a labour of love and everything in the house was handcrafted, including the tiles on the roof, the doors and windows. It had a neat mezzanine with an entry window tucked away in the clerestory that could be accessed through a ladder from the courtyard. In the words of the two brothers, '*Yeh ghar mitti se bana hai aur mitti me jaayega.* (This house is made of earth and will go back to the earth.)' The house and their narratives were a goldmine. I saw the technique of rammed earth construction and the by-product of their rice crop serving as anti-termite treatment. The charpoys were woven using ropes made of leaves from the nearby forest, and locally available white clay was used to plaster the earthen walls. In today's parlance we hear the terms 'sustainability' and 'circular economy' being bandied about. What better example than this can there be of a cradle-to-cradle (a term made popular by William McDonough and Michael Braungart) approach?[28]

The value of documenting oral histories dawned on me. My mind was abuzz with ideas. There was a dire need to record this wisdom for posterity. Could we build an app or a website where people could upload such information as videos, sketches or essays and make it openly accessible to all? Would the Ministry of Culture, Government of India, be interested in encouraging such a project if I initiated it? Would our community of architects and colleges of design come together to make this repository? After all, this knowledge will be of use to us. With the rate at which transformation was occurring in our built spaces across the country, such wisdom would soon become obsolete unless we paid heed to it. These invisible monuments are our

---

[28]McDonough, William, and Michael Braungart, *Cradle to Cradle: Remaking the Way We Make Things*, North Point Press, New York, NY, 22 April 2002.

heritage and we need to find ways to preserve at least the know-how to build them.

A large section of our population does not live in the pristine homes that architects design. Most design and build themselves, using and honing their home-grown wisdom as they do. It is time we start paying attention to commonplace buildings. These spaces have an immense wealth of knowledge to share, many tales to tell, and show a sensible path for the future—our future. This is an ode to the monuments that we pass by every day, the ones usually not spared a second look. They are precious to the narrative of our land as they form the spine of our collective lifestyle. They are what should inform our culture at large.

Here's to the invisible monuments—the ones that house the soul of India!

With 80-year-old Jashoda near Dholpur in Rajasthan

Day 68—With Haryana Police officials at the Office of the Commissioner of Police in Faridabad

Top: *Commemorative walk from Raj Ghat to Red Fort in New Delhi*
Bottom: *With supporters post the commemorative walk*

En route to Delhi

Stretching post-walk

Conversing with locals along the way

En route to Dhaka in Bangladesh

Walking over the Madhumati Bridge in Bangladesh

CHAPTER 30

MILESTONES

The first 100 km seems paltry when I now look back at the entire journey. But when I completed my first century in less than four days, it was indeed a special achievement for me and my team. I completed 500 km within the border of Jharkhand and shared my excitement with some policemen who happened to be walking with me at that point. Meeting these milestones gave me the courage and the energy to get to the next.

I still remember the 1,000-kilometre milestone vividly. It was a big deal. I ran the last 500 metres and melted into my husband's arms, sobbing. These were tears of joy and I felt a tremendous sense of achievement. It was the 39th day and I had walked a whopping 1,000 km in all.

In the moments that followed, I silently thanked the many people who had supported me and dear friends who had kept me company through phone calls and helped me tide through trying times. I spoke to my mother who had called me every day to hear about my struggles. My on-ground and back-end team celebrated. I sent a WhatsApp broadcast to all my friends who were keeping a close watch on my journey. I was overwhelmed and sank into quietude for the rest of the day until I reached my destination.

The 1,500-kilometre landmark did not evoke as many emotions, though the team had organized a cake for me to cut. This 1,500-kilometre mark happened after the disastrous fall in Gwalior and should have been a moment of great relief, but my eyes were set on the remaining 200 km and I had begun to count backwards.

I started following milestones on the highway. They announced the distances to my destination. Milestones on national highways are painted with a yellow band on top, state highways have green bands, those on city or district main roads have blue or black bands and those on village routes have orange bands. As children, our father would take us on road trips and we delighted in keeping tabs on distances through these milestones. On this journey, I was often grossly fooled by the figures on them. There was one particular occasion when I knew that Jhansi was over 425 km away, while the yellow and white stones by the side of the road read 311 km. It was akin to a mirage of an oasis in a desert.

As I was nearing Delhi, I was keen on reaching the point that said 100 km to Delhi so that I could get a photograph of myself taken next to the sign. Finally, when we discovered this precious milestone, we found it had fallen to the ground, probably because of a road accident. I went ahead and took that picture and labelled it: 'Breaking the 100-kilometre milestone!'

Milestones on this trip were of different kinds. Every time I broke my record for the number of kilometres in a day, moving from 26, 28, 30, 32, 34, 36 and then to 40 km, each day felt like a milestone. Another incredible feeling was when I crossed over to another state— seven such milestones in all! Entering Jharkhand from West Bengal on a bridge over the Subarnarekha River as the sun was rising behind me made me feel euphoric. Even before I crossed over, I began noticing how the landscape changed, from flat to hilly, as I walked through Purulia district. But once I crossed over, I started feeling it in my limbs. It was two days of walking from Ranchi and I had 410 metres of altitude to bridge. Hence, the steep climbs in Jharkhand were huge achievements too, especially when I saw Garmin (my smartwatch) galloping away to approximately 110 floors of climbing, a total ascent of 327 metres in one day.

Every time I was able to convey the role of design to people or when I felt that they knew or understood what an architect does, it felt like a notable achievement for me. Piquing people's interest and getting them to share their stories with me every day was my goal and I found immense satisfaction each time I could have a conversation.

The day I started going to bed without throbbing pain in my limbs was also a special day. The day I walked in the rain, the first time I walked at night, the first time I lay down under a tree in the wilderness and shut my eyes, the first local school I visited, the first village community I spent time in, the first formal and informal interactions were all milestones that made this journey full of intrigue, discovery and fulfilment.

CHAPTER 31

HARYANA: AB DILLI DOOR NAHIN

Day 67 to Day 70
20 April 2022 to 23 April 2022

I had entered Haryana, the penultimate state on this journey, and I could confidently quote: '*Ab Dilli door nahin* (now Delhi is not far)!' This is also the title of a movie produced by the legendary Raj Kapoor, first released in 1957. Set in 1951, it portrayed the hardships of a poor family living in a remote village. The young son walks to Delhi to meet the then Prime Minister Jawaharlal Nehru, seeking justice for his father on death row. More recently, another film of the same name has been released, inspired by the real-life story of the son of a rickshaw puller, Govind Jaiswal, who became an IAS officer in 2007. This slogan has now come to have political connotations and implies that the power at the centre is accessible.

However, for me, this slogan was not figurative but real. Along the way, many used this phrase with me, and I had to grin and reply, '*Dilli abhi bahut door hai* (Delhi is still very far away).' Now that I was less than 50 km from the border, I could say it out loud without getting jinxed.

I was almost there.

It was a short passage through Palwal and Faridabad in Haryana. From the religious centre that is Mathura, the transformation to the industrial zone of Haryana was quite pronounced. Gone were the quaint hamlets. I was firmly on the expressways of development yet again. There was a marked change in the temperature of the surroundings, and the heat was compounded by the lack of trees. I experienced the heat island effect first-hand. Construction was underway all along the way and this came with all the trappings of construction material, debris, shanties and pollution.

Nothing of what used to be the way of life a few decades ago was on display.

Showstopper 35

With Mathura and Vrindavan not being too far away, religion still played an important role in people's lives. I encountered another strong woman, Lali, who seemed to be in her 70s. A widow, she lived all by herself, although she had two daughters and four sons, all of whom were married and settled. We reached her home and found it to be a good place to rest, but we saw no one around. On calling through the open door, she hobbled out and told us about how she was unwell and that her neighbours were taking care of her.

This was another common norm that we saw. The community functioned as a family and took care of their own. The neighbouring women also joined us for a chat. Hearing about my expedition, Lali excitedly told us about the 84 Kos Yatra that she had undertaken a few years ago (kos is a unit of measurement and is equal to 3 km).

The 252-kilometre journey is usually completed over a period of seven days and covers twelve forests (or vans), twenty ponds (kunds) and many religious destinations associated with the kingdom of Lord Rama. It is popular faith that undertaking this journey frees a person from the obligation of completing 8.4 million lifetimes. When asked why Lali undertook this pilgrimage and if it was in gratitude for the fulfilment of prayer, she shrugged her shoulders and said it was a trip to see India. She had travelled alone but made acquaintances along the way as she walked. She was close to seventy when she undertook this trip!

I quizzed her on the diet that kept her fit, which turned out to be jaggery, ghee, milk and sugarcane! Her eyesight is sharp and she can thread a needle comfortably even today. We also chatted about the benefits of using earthenware utensils, cooking on a slow flame and eating fresh food, seasonal vegetables and a good quantity of lentils and pulses. She spoke of how sitting cross-legged on the floor and working in the fields had helped her stay agile.

When speaking of kos as a unit of distance, kos minars naturally follow. These are solid round pillars of brick masonry around 30 feet high and plastered over with lime. I was introduced to kos minars by Khushwant Sharma, a young architect who graduated in 2018. He joined me as I walked through Palwal, his home town. Kos minars are mediaeval Indian milestones along the Grand Trunk Road introduced by the ruler Sher Shah Suri. The King undertook repairs of Chandragupta's Royal Road in the sixteenth century. The original Royal Road, built in the third century BCE, was planned to have trees and wells at every half kos, with enough rest houses for weary travellers along the route. Sher Shah Suri increased the number of wells and trees while adding gardens for relief too. The state of Haryana has the highest number of kos minars and they are in a relatively better state as well.

Being over 6 feet tall, Khushwant easily matched my pace. At one point, he noticed that I was quickening my strides and quipped that he only needed to take longer strides and that three of my strides were equal to his giant step. This is a problem I have always faced—the need for a high cadence to keep a good pace. There are times when I have had to pound 250 steps to a minute when running to keep up a good pace, while the average cadence is between 150–180 steps per minute. So, walking close to 10 km with me was actually a walk in the park for Khushwant.

We used this time together to exchange notes and he told me about himself. He chose to set up his practice in the small town of Palwal as his family was here; his responsibilities included maintaining agricultural land while managing his practice. Palwal, or any small town in India, does not lend itself easily to a thriving architectural practice, so most of his projects were based out of Delhi, Faridabad and other cities. It all came down to the respect common people had for the profession and the economics of hiring an architect. Our law currently does not prevent anyone from performing the role of an architect—only the use of the title 'architect' is regulated. In such a scenario, if people get easy designs and drawings from non-architects at a much lower price, they would shun the services of an actual architect. The value that an architect brings through design to better lives and reduce costs needs to be communicated widely. Khushwant compared the profession of architecture to divinity, wherein architects have the power to create environments that impact well-being.

The last gathering of architects—to welcome me and hear my story—was hosted in Faridabad by the IIA Haryana Chapter. I thank my friend and senior from college, Punit Sethi, the Chapter Chairman, for inviting me to share my journey.

Walking through Haryana brought a kind of numbness in my emotions as I neared my destination. Another couple of days and this euphoria would end; the joy had been in the journey, and that was soon coming to a close.

CHAPTER 32

THE AGONIES AND THE ECSTASIES

Mitch Albom, in his book, *Five People You Meet in Heaven,* says, 'All endings are also beginnings. We just don't know it at the time.'[29]

Who among those that I passed every day or spent a short duration with would I meet again during my lifetime? Would any of them be among the five I meet in my afterlife? Every time I connected with someone through a namaste, a handshake, a smile, a chat or even simply through silence, I was changed as a person. This included my engagement with the soul-stirring sights of nature that my eyes beheld. Every moment of the walk made me grateful for everything and everyone in my life. Hand-in-hand were the joys of learning from their contented lives and the heartache of leaving the people I met behind, knowing that I would probably never come across them again.

Irving Stone, in his masterpiece *The Agony and the Ecstasy,*[30] describes Michelangelo's journey as he created his magnum opus, the Sistine Chapel ceiling. Well, this 1700 was my magnum opus. I crafted it with care and it came with its share of agonies and ecstasies. The planning stages saw people believing in me and accepting partnerships and pledging contributions, but many requests for support did not come through. Help that came from unexpected quarters certainly gave the necessary fillip to our enthusiasm during our planning days. The efforts of Ravi Sarangan, an architect and a special friend, led to Mahindra First Choice loaning us a Scorpio for our journey. Our team was on a high the day the industrialist, Anand Mahindra, reposted

[29]Albom, Mitch, *The Five People You Meet In Heaven,* Hachette Books, New York, NY, 7 April 2003.
[30]Stone, Irving, *The Agony and the Ecstasy: A Biographical Novel of Michelangelo,* Berkeley, CA, 7 September 2004.

my tweet about my journey on Day 53[31]; I was then merely 318 km away from Delhi. This tweet was picked up by some vernacular newspapers as well, and one of them even claimed that I had already reached Delhi when I still had seventeen days to go.

I had arrived!

There were so many times on this journey when I felt the truth of Carl Sagan's words, 'The cosmos is within us. We are made of star-stuff.'[32] We are a way for the universe to know itself. How else do I explain what made me wake up at 3 a.m. every day for 70 days and set out on a test of physical endurance that I did not know I was ever built for? How did I, someone who is extremely possessive about my chair at the dining table, my bed, my side of the bed, my toilet, my towel, my way in the kitchen, suddenly undergo such a makeover, almost overnight, so that none of these things were on my mind?

As I laid out my mat for my post-walk stretches in a temple complex on the banks of the Tamas River, across the dilapidated Madhavgarh Fort, and followed it with a chat with a priest from the Hanuman temple, how could my mind even dwell on the hardships of my journey? My aches and pains dissipated, and I revelled in the joy of discovery. The fifty-five-year-old priest, Rajmanik Pande, had been officiating at this temple for close to forty years, following in the footsteps of his father and grandfather. He proudly spoke about how his sanctum had been recently embellished with orange ceramic tiles by a benefactor and was easier to maintain. I lamented the sad reality of the state of design awareness and aesthetic appreciation in mass culture.

I felt a searing bolt strike at me every time I heard and learned that designers and architects do not exist in the minds of the common people at large. I often heard of our field of design being termed as 'niche'. Our world fails or thrives on design. We engage with design

---

[31]Tweet that Ananda Mahindra reposted: https://twitter.com/gita_ethos/status/1511316754827743241?lang=ar, which was also shared by news publications such as *Aaj Tak Kolkata, Janta Se Rishta, Patrika.com* and *Ei Muhurte* on 6 April 2022.
[32]*Cosmos: A Spacetime Odyssey* is a 2014 American science documentary television series, which was presented by Carl Sagan on the Public Broadcasting Service and is considered a milestone for scientific documentaries.

almost every moment of our lives, and yet the field is slotted as a niche. Possibly, over 80 per cent of an average human's life is spent in enclosed spaces. The more I walked and interacted with people, spaces and architecture, the more I was convinced that architects need to be a lot more visible in our communities. Our responsibility does not end within the boundaries of our sites. Every choice we make within that boundary has a far-reaching implication on the lives of the likes of Sumari—the brick kiln worker's daughter; Ram Lakhan—who turns from a construction worker in the city to a contractor in his village; and Rajmanik Pande—the priest who was delighted with orange tiles for his temple walls.

We are responsible for the trends and aspirations of people. Anjali from Bishnupur says that she knows that earthen homes are better for thermal comfort and that she will still build her new home with modern materials as people around her are making the same choices. When buildings made of mud and thatch or tiles carry the tag of 'kachcha', meaning temporary, anyone building afresh will want to move towards 'pucca', meaning permanence. My conversations with women revealed that they bore the brunt of the problems that came with poor maintenance of their homes—leaks, pest infestation and other structural disrepair. Regular maintenance meant resources, skills, time and money. They preferred to put up with the discomfort with respect to ventilation and thermal well-being and even gave up on the aesthetic pleasure that their earlier homes had bestowed.

If only the change was limited to just that. The way buildings and spaces are designed and carved has huge consequences on the way people live. There are drastic changes in lifestyle. I witnessed these changes sadly. I noticed interactions diminishing and even disappearing in regions where the walls of houses or compound walls extended to the edge of the site as there were no platforms or threshold spaces to invite discussion between homes. The feeling of community seemed to dissolve and the dynamics of a vibrant, interactive, cooperative society underwent a paradigm shift with these new constructions. It was almost as if these walls extended into the minds of the people who lived in these locales. I saw fewer smiles, nods and cheerful banter. That is the power of design. It can make, break, facilitate and change.

Paul Goldberger, a famous critic of architecture, once said, 'Social responsibility in architecture is, at least in part, a matter of believing, passionately and absolutely, in the potential of architecture to improve the quality of life.'[33] A socially responsible attitude while practising architecture is essential for socially responsive trends to take place.

---

[33]'Does Architecture Matter? Thoughts on Social Responsibility, Buildings, and the World After September 11th', *Paul Goldberger*, 8 October 2002, https:// www.paulgoldberger.com/lectures/does-architecture-matter-thoughts-on-social-responsibility-buildings-and-the-world-after-september-11th/. Accessed on 4 January 2024.

Walk,
to touch.
Walk,
to bridge.
Walk,
to change.
Walk,
to be changed.
Walk,
and you shall achieve!

CHAPTER 33

IT'S OVER

24 April 2022

I had already entered Delhi the day before, on Day 69. As we started our journey from the Faridabad side of the border at 5 a.m., we thought Delhi was only 3 km away. It warmed my heart to see four friends waiting at the starting point to join me in this special moment—M.K. Sunil, a batchmate from architecture school, had flown in from Bengaluru to spend this once-in-a-lifetime moment with me; V. Krishnamurthy, a business associate from the past; Divya Kush, former President of IIA was there with his wife, Lata. Nikita and Rasya from Team Ethos came in hopping, skipping and jumping in joy, and we hugged warmly.

The moment of crossing over to Delhi was anticlimactic. No one knew where Haryana ended and Delhi started as there were no boards on the route! We suddenly began noticing boards mentioning Delhi and then started asking around. At a toll gate, the staff told us that Delhi had begun, but someone else mentioned that the Badarpur Border Metro Station was where Delhi began. Yet another person insisted that there was a board marking its beginning on the flyover, which I missed. I did a few takes for the camera, where I seem to be crossing over to Delhi at different locations, and we had footage of all these places. Delhi had arrived somewhere along the way, and I didn't know.

We assumed that the toll gate was the border, and Bala had arranged a video call with the kids: Pranav, Shreya and Gaurav. They were also able to join me during these emotional final moments.

We had decided that this occasion would be a gathering of all the people working behind the scenes and on the ground—they had planned everything to the smallest detail and were the reason that this journey had been without any hiccups. As Ethos was a virtual office, some colleagues were meeting each other for the first time, and so the union was even sweeter. The back-end team had already arrived on Day 69, and we met at a restaurant to plan the last lap of the 1700. Some from the team later confessed that they were disappointed by my reaction, or the lack of it when I met them. There was none. They expected to see me on a high and instead encountered a rather quiet Gita. But what can I say, I was still focused on meticulously planning the next day! It took many days for the magnitude of what I had achieved to sink in.

But, as we began the last lap at Raj Ghat at 6.45 a.m., jubilation seemed to be in the air. I walked back and forth to keep different people company—some who had been mentors in their own way at different points of my life, others who had been keenly following the 1700 and were excited to be part of this final lap to Red Fort, and some others who were strangers and had learned of my journey through their friends. I was overjoyed that Shravan, one of my four confidantes from the start, had travelled from Chennai to be with me for the last lap. Rajiv Ahir and Dharmarajan also joined in with their families, which meant a lot as three of the four people I brainstormed on this impossible idea before I started even believing I could do it were there with me as it came to a close. I looked at the motley group of almost a hundred supporters who had come together and felt blessed.

At 7.15 a.m., we were at the Red Fort. The journey had concluded!

The team was already there, celebrating the conclusion of this epic initiative. Friends who had come together dispersed to carry out their Sunday plans—a breakfast at Chandni Chowk, a music concert in the evening, a lunch at their favourite restaurant, cuddling with a book in a favourite corner at home, a game of tennis—I imagined.

As realization dawned that it had ended, I let out an involuntary gasp. I was richer for the experience, but I felt extremely deprived as well, for I would never again feel the way I felt as I walked the 1700. There will certainly be more expeditions, but none will evoke the emotions of the first.

We were staying at the India International Centre. I felt a deep vacuum within me as I returned to my erstwhile life. Nothing was different and everything was different. I planned to stay in Delhi for a few days before I returned to Kolkata; Bala had left after a day. We snatched a few quiet moments together, sitting in silence. Over those first few days, I found myself weeping without knowing why. Why was I comfortable in the company of strangers, but awkward with people I knew? The question would inevitably pop up about the trip, making me recede into myself.

Through the last seventy days, I had depended on Vinayak for all my expenditures. I carried no currency and no credit cards. On the 1700, I had felt like the child who jumps with absolutely no fear when asked to jump, in total confidence that a safe pair of hands awaited her. After bidding farewell to Bala as he left for the airport, I walked up to Khan Market to treat myself to a sumptuous breakfast. Breakfast had been one of my most frugal of meals over the past seventy days. I was presented the bill at the charming restaurant, The Blue Door Cafe, and I froze. I realized I had no money on me, nor any mode of payment activated on my phone. Panicking, I dialled Bala and was thankful when he answered the call. He had boarded and the flight was almost about to leave, but I heaved a sigh of relief as he quickly completed the payment on my behalf.

What should I do now that the journey was over? How could I slip back into the old normal? How did I get out of an addiction to physical exertion, of being a constant presence on social media even while being rather alone? In many ways, my return to normal life felt like a rebirth. I felt a tremendous resistance from within to many things that I had to get back to. I found it hard to get into modes of transportation, particularly when the commute was less than 5 km. I was clocking 10–15 km a day for many days even after I returned home as I chose to walk to most places. My need to walk made me the butt of many jokes. There were people who asked me if I was planning to walk back from Delhi to Kolkata too. When I had problems with excess baggage on the return flight, people joked that my feet were more reliable and that I should use them.

On my return, I was eager to get back to my bed and thought

that I would sleep like a baby; but I found myself tossing, turning and groaning after a few hours. For at least a couple of months after I returned, I struggled with back pain as I changed positions when sleeping. It was strange. It took me a while to figure out the cause: my body was no longer used to lying down for long hours! The longest I slept at a stretch on the 1700 had probably been six hours, and I usually slept far less. I did try to catch up with a catnap in the afternoon, but even cats do not sleep when they are high on adrenaline. Regular back exercises and time helped me overcome the back pain.

I thought I would take time off from work and slowly settle in, but I had to dive back in immediately. There were too many things to be done! Accounts had to be settled, acknowledgements and notes of gratitude had to be sent out. I was invited by various organizations, institutions, schools and colleges to speak about my journey. I remember the first felicitation from my alma mater, SPA, Delhi, the day after we touched the Red Fort. I stood on the same stage where we had performed on our freshers' night and shared my experience. I was touched by the efforts that the college had taken to acknowledge my feat. The students had painted a larger-than-life mural of me, and there were many selfies sought.

Now that it was over, the journey loomed large behind me and ahead of me too. In a conversation with a friend, a cancer survivor, I remember mentioning that I had taken things one day at a time while walking the 1700; that is what got me through it and made it so full of joy. She responded that she had done the same thing while she was going through her cancer treatment. One day at a time. In fact, maybe even one moment at a time.

The first month after I returned, I felt like I was walking on a cloud. I felt very light and unaffected by most things. I was in a stupor most of the time, even as I was writing reports, penning down my thoughts, leaving voice notes to myself and planning for the future. I found ideas originating from deep within, and the passion I felt for all the things that I was planning was of a different intensity. I was as honest as before, but my understanding had changed. The few months after the 1700 were surely the most fertile of my life. I was brimming with peace, love and purpose.

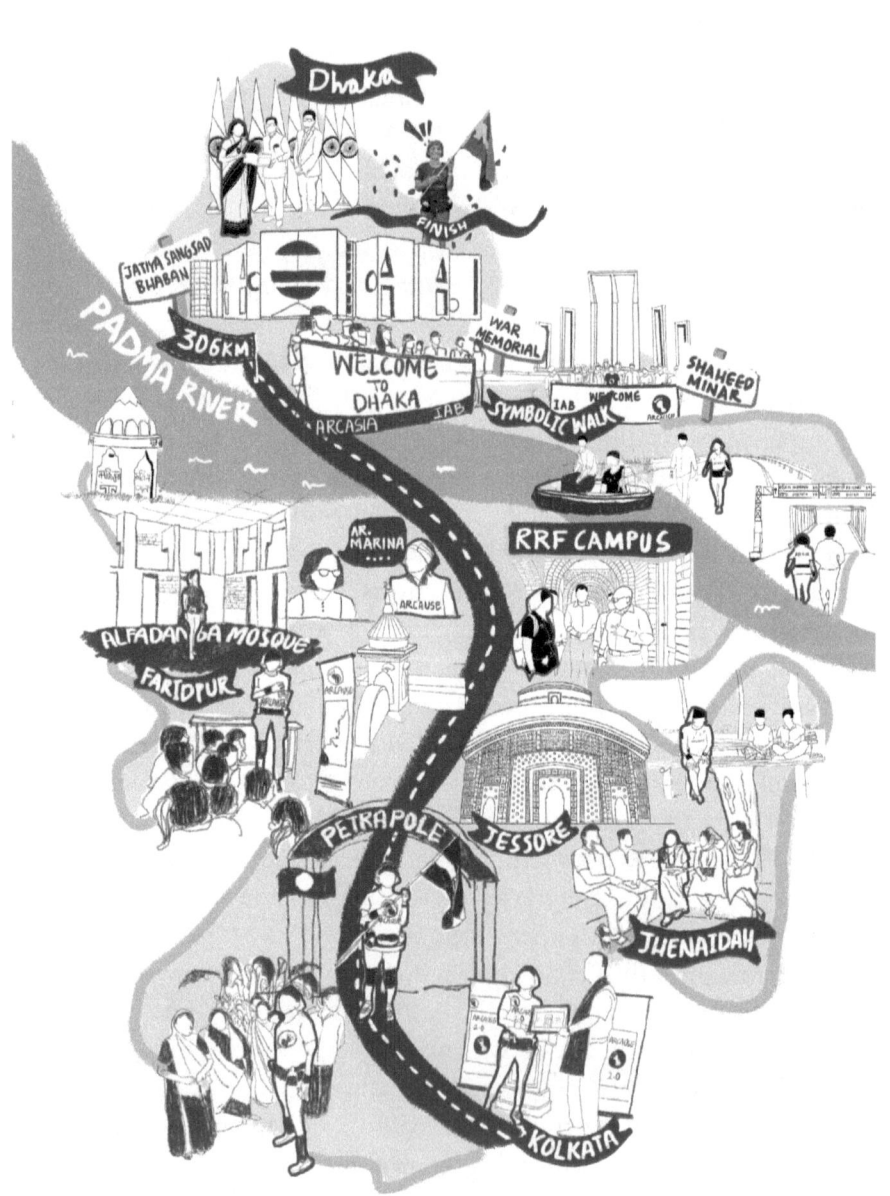

CHAPTER 34

WALK FOR ARCAUSE 2.0—
KOLKATA TO DHAKA

22 October 2022 to 7 November 2022

Over a couple of months after the first walk, I gradually slipped into a new normal. We consolidated the discoveries of the walk, made reports and curated two fellowships (where young designers were to be picked to work on real-life projects that needed design interventions). Plenty had been planned and there was a lot to look forward to. And yet, I was restless. I had sipped elixir, and my heart yearned for more, which led to the conceptualization of Walk for Arcause 2.0—Kolkata to Dhaka: Architects Without Borders.

The team was in a tizzy once again. Anushree and Aiswarya, who had been part of the first walk, had moved on, so the back-end team was built again, with Akshatha and Vaishnavi, led by Sonam and Rasya. Vinayak and Param from the first edition joined me on this adventure too, the former managing logistics and taking pictures on his phone, while the latter continued his role of taking videos and stills with his camera. We were to take our personal car to India's border and had made arrangements for a car and driver to meet us on the other side of the border.

July 2022 was the genesis of this walk across borders when I was invited to Jaipur by Tushar Sogani, the chairman of IIA, Rajasthan Chapter, as a speaker at the Rajasthan Architecture Festival. Architects from different parts of the subcontinent were present. The President of ARCASIA (Architects Regional Council, Asia), Dr Abu Sayeed M. Ahmed, and renowned architects from Bangladesh, Marina Tabassum and Qazi Arif, were also present. This is where the idea of a walk from Kolkata to Dhaka germinated. It was suggested that it should coincide with the fiftieth anniversary celebrations of the Institute of Architects Bangladesh.

As this was to be a walk across national borders, it needed to be planned differently. I started by contacting the Bangladesh Deputy High Commission in Kolkata. After a few emails and phone calls, the Deputy High Commissioner, Mr Andalib Elias, invited me to his chamber. He had a quizzical expression when I spoke about walking to Dhaka. Many questions and a cup of tea later, he was very enthused about this mission: uniting through design. He was keen that we flag off this 'padajatra' from the Deputy High Commission itself. He generously offered to host a breakfast for the guests who were to see me set off. I was taken around the building and the historical importance of the edifice came to light. This was where the first embassy of Bangladesh was set up after the 1971 war when Bangladesh gained its independence from Pakistan.

I had to brush up on my history. As Bangladesh was a neighbour to our nation and its origins were so closely entangled with India's, I needed to know it all. Surbhit Lihala, a co-runner, introduced me to the book, *The Vortex: A True Story of History's Deadliest Storm, an Unspeakable War, and Liberation*, authored by Scott Carney and Jason Miklian.[34] The book narrates the course that 'The Great Bhola Cyclone', one of the deadliest storms in history, took in November 1970 when it ripped through the country, rending it into two, and bringing the world to the brink of nuclear war. This storm, an event caused by climate change, led to the loss of over 5,00,000 lives and set off a chain of events, with political chicanery taking centre stage. The result was a most gruesome war and a genocide, in which millions of Bangladeshis, then citizens of East Pakistan, were butchered. Through these agonizing birth pangs, Bangladesh was born in 1971.

It was indeed a coincidence that as I was flagged off on 22 October 2022 from the Deputy High Commission, another storm was brewing—she was named Sitrang and was expected to land on

---

[34]Carney, Scott, and Jason Miklian, *The Vortex: A True Story of History's Deadliest Storm, an Unspeakable War, and Liberation*, HarperCollins, New York, NY, 29 March 2022.

25 October. It gave me goosebumps when it occurred to me that I would be walking the same route that so many refugees (those who had then made homes at Salt Lake, Kolkata, years ago) had used to return to their land once their country was free. My border crossing was planned to take place on 26 October and I had decided to take a rest day on 24 October to give the team a holiday on Diwali, but we had to rejig our plans to beat Sitrang. I walked on a wet Diwali morning and chose to lay low on the day the cyclone was to enter. We need not have worried so much. Sitrang, fortunately, turned out to be a damp squib. We marched on through Barasat, Chandpara and Bangaon. In West Bengal, Diwali is celebrated as Kali Puja, and it is grander than Durga Puja in some districts; I was exhilarated to walk through some of them. The colourful alpona (rangoli-like artistic patterns) on the temple grounds, housing complexes and homes were a sight to behold.

The roads got narrower and were lined with huge canopies of trees—mahogany, shisham, shirish. It was a glorious stretch of 60 km, a poet's delight. Around five years ago, there had been a move to cut about 4,000 of these trees to make way for a four-lane highway. We read that a protest by many youths, similar to a mini Chipko movement, had taken place at that time. I am glad to only have seen a two-lane highway for most of this route, on which the India–Bangladesh Greenline bus sped to reach its destination.

On my earlier walk, I had been walking westward and the sun had been behind me. Here it was straight ahead, framed by the trees. The ball of red had an uncanny similarity to the circle on the Bangladesh flag, which I was carrying with me as a token of friendship for my architect friends across the border. Mr Andalib Elias had kindly arranged for one at my request.

And finally, I was at the coveted moment of this trip—the border crossing. I was at Petrapole. Ar. Charanjit Shah was the architect of the new immigration terminal building, which is a massive complex and was then under construction. He offered me a site visit. Rohit Kumar, a young architect from his site office, gave me a short tour. I stood there, imagining how this place would be transformed once this building would be fully operational.

I proudly ran in, waving the national flag towards the current immigration building. As we were travelling by car, our belongings were scattered in multiple small bags and we were stumped at the counters; trolleys are allowed only up to a point and we had to carry the bags once we had finished immigration. Vinayak and Param graciously urged me to carry what I could with my two hands and move on while they managed the rest. I took two bags on wheels, one handbag and a backpack, and set off. As I got out of the building, it dawned on me that the hour I had spent getting formalities done at the official Indian counters would now have to be repeated on the Bangladesh side. I was leaving one country and entering another. There were forms to fill out, IDs to be verified, COVID certificates to be checked and questions to be answered before I was let into our neighbouring country, all this after I had walked 28 km. Thanks to my attire, curiosity took the lead. I was asked if I was an athlete or a sportsperson. When they learned of my mission, all the officials and support staff present made every attempt to make the transition an easy one. There were more selfies taken too. An hour or less later, which seemed like an eternity (thanks to the bags that I was lugging), I was in Benapole.

My friend, the architect Shahrear Rehman, whom I had met only virtually so far, was there with a reporter from a Bangladesh daily to receive me. I was relieved to have located our car and driver, Kamrul, who was to navigate us from this point to Dhaka. I found a TV reporter waiting for me too. He interviewed me, and this was the first time I had to respond completely in Bengali! My grasp of the language had improved immensely over my walks, but the Bangladeshi dialect was quite different and it made it harder for me to casually communicate. I was repeatedly told in all my interactions with the press and with people too that they found my diction to be very musical and sweet. I am sure they were only being polite and that was their way of conveying to me that my Bengali needed more work.

Quite a crowd gathered around me. News of an Indian woman walking her way to Dhaka spread like wildfire. Evidence of this revealed itself over the next week as people recognized me and wanted to chat and take pictures all the way to the capital.

I reached our hotel well before Vinayak and Param because they had been tasked with bringing all the other bags, changing currency and getting local SIM cards for our phones. I did rest but I could barely sleep while they were dead to the world for a few hours after they checked into the accommodation. The manager of the hotel, with whom I had tea, told me about his family in Barisal, 200 km away. He was leading a bachelor's life to earn his livelihood. He promised to wave me off the next morning, but I had a feeling that he would not, considering the unearthly hour I had planned to set out.

I was also visited by representatives of the local police station that evening; they wanted information on our schedule, our route and our contact details. They took it upon themselves to keep a tab on my safety as I was a guest in their country. Sure enough, we were provided with numbers to reach out to in case of emergencies. Police officers met with us at different points throughout the journey. Although I was on an unusual journey and in an unknown land, I felt safe.

It did take a little getting used to though. As I set off from Benapole in the early hours, the first part of the route took me through a bus stand and a road where many trucks were parked. I encountered people who looked a little different due to their attire and, maybe also their body language. I found that they were staring, but I was used to this. I began smiling at them and found that their faces, which I thought looked rather stern earlier, would soften with smiles and grins. That helped break the ice. And lo, I was in my groove again! 'Salam alaykums' replaced the 'namastes' and I was back to making friends. Bangladesh surprised me, pleasantly though. The route passed through Laujani, Narail, Jessore, Bhanga and then Dhaka. I had so far only visited Dhaka and here I was walking in the hinterlands. What a difference! The theme for this Walk for Arcause 2.0 was unity through design. This rang true for me in many ways on this journey.

I observed unity in design in the lives of the people where the violation of one element may mean that the entire ecosystem is in danger. People understood that it is important for everyone to collaborate to retain the richness of their lifestyles. For instance, they needed to be united in valuing the river and waterbodies as their lifeline for the community to survive together. I also saw many craft guilds (rare these days), and there appeared to be a togetherness in their practice of the craft and in their marketing too.

Showstopper 36

Marina Tabassum thoughtfully introduced me to Hasibul Kabir, winner of the Aga Khan Award for the Jhenaidah River Front Project.[35] I took a detour by car to spend a night at Jhenaidah and understand how the design of the riverfront had united the community. This is a community-driven project providing public spaces in a riverine city with 2,50,000 residents, offering walkways, gardens and cultural facilities, as well as environmental efforts to increase biodiversity along the river. I was taken around the project by Sakib, who represented the Citywide Peoples Network of Jhenaidah.

Kabir was travelling at the time. Besides visiting his office, I was invited for an evening of interaction and music with the community responsible for the project. The evening was made so much more special with songs of Lalon sung by some locals. I was absolutely delighted when I asked Sakib who the winner of the award was and pat came his reply: 'The process.' Seeing the motley group of community members, which included people from various backgrounds—accountants, a swimming coach, a maths teacher, housewives and college-going students—all of whom were responsible for the design and execution of the project, it was clear that the process of bringing them together had been key.

Narail, one of the districts that fell en route, is well-known for S.M. Sultan, a Bengali decolonial artist who hailed from here. His style was specific, with exaggerated dictions of the muscular features of peasants of his country. Mashrafe Mortuza, who has served as the captain of the Bangladeshi cricket team, was born in Narail. Closer home, Narail was also the birthplace of Suvra Mukherjee, the former First Lady of India, and the wife of the former President of India, Pranab Mukherjee.

---

[35]Afzal, Farhat, 'Winners Receive Aga Khan Award for Architecture at the 2022 Ceremony', *Context*, 31 October 2022, https://contextbd.com/winners-receive-aga-khan-awards-for-architecture-at-the-2022-ceremony/. Accessed on 4 January 2024.

Showstopper 37

I am grateful to Shahrear for suggesting that I stay at the premises of the Rural Reconstruction Foundation (RRF) at Jessore. This NGO was set up in 1982 by Father Philip Biswas and his wife, Rita Biswas. RRF works for the domain of social and economic emancipation of underprivileged people. They have set up a training and research centre with the objective of imparting skills to rural people so they can improve their lives. The campus, designed by Sayedul Hasan Rana, was a haven of peace. The exposed brick and concrete gave it an unassuming aesthetic, which also conveyed great sensitivity and allure; the architect had cleverly interplayed the open and built spaces. The large veranda outside my room was my refuge to do nothing but sit and stare.

Hari, the caretaker, played his role so well as a host. In a casual conversation, he figured out my preferences for vegetables and ensured that I tasted everything that I liked during the two days that I was there. As a vegetarian, I was apprehensive of what I would encounter in a nation dominated by Muslims, known for their partiality to non-vegetarian cuisine. Vegetarian Bengalis are a rarity even back home in West Bengal. Again, Bangladesh surprised me. The region that I walked through was rich in vegetables and rural households certainly cooked much vegetarian fare, along with fish.

Showstopper 38

I was forewarned about the hospitality in Bangladesh and I did get an opportunity to experience this quite often. In Jhenaidah, we were treated to a fabulous vegetarian lunch at Alamgir Kabir and Selina Akter's house. There were over thirty dishes, and the warmth and simplicity of the couple and their home made my eyes well up. Kabir is a mathematics teacher at the local school and he takes it upon himself to inculcate a curiosity for science and maths in the children of his community. He had a bio-flocculation well in his backyard and was building a multi-storeyed pen for his goat and poultry, putting it together with the children and youth around. He had even made a mud and bamboo model to understand the intricacies of building such a structure.

Showstopper 39

Similarly, the hospitality at Buraich Maulvi Bari is certainly something to write about. I was advised to stay at this heritage home belonging to the family of a Maulvi by Marina Tabassum and Abu Sayeed. The latter had been involved in the restoration of the project, while the former had built the mosque in the forecourt of the house. We were among the first guests to stay in this four-bedroom homestay that tempted you to enjoy its simple interiors by day and mesmerize you with its simple lighting by night. The sounds of the village added to its charm. The mosque, which had just been completed and was not yet commissioned, appeared to follow the sun, and the patterns created by the light and shadow made for a lot of drama. I could imagine devotees having favourite places at different times of the day in this mosque—as they must do in many other buildings that Marina has designed.

Coming back to the hospitality, the food that was served here was delicious too. I had heard about bhortas, a famous dish, before I left for the nation. In India, we have often eaten bhartas of potato and brinjal. To give a better idea, a bharta or bhorta of potatoes is not too different from mashed potatoes. In Alfadanga, we were served at least five bhortas with every meal, made with runner beans, broad beans, kala jeera (black caraway), tomatoes, pumpkin and many other vegetables. Alfadanga, a quiet village involved in jute cultivation, sits in the Faridpur district and it lived up to its reputation, encompassed in the popular saying, 'Faridpur hospitality can kill.' It did kill all our hunger and left us smiling silly with full bellies after every meal.

The story of this walk would not be complete if I were to miss mentioning two young architecture students—Prasenjit Sarkar Anik from Khulna University and Shaneworne Mukherjee from Bangabandhu Sheikh Mujibur Rahman Science and Technology University, Gopalganj. Yes, you read that right. However, this Shaneworne does not play cricket but enjoys football. Shaneworne was named after the famous cricketer, Shane Warne, and is often the object of many jokes. In fact, when Shane Warne passed away, many of his classmates contacted our young Shaneworne to enquire about his well-being. His brother was named Waynerooney, but his name was changed a few years later. Shaneworne and Prasenjit are sensible young men with pleasing demeanours. They were great company and gave me an insight into the lives of the people of this countryside. I learnt from them about the well-designed and colourful 'daan bakshas'—donation boxes located on the roadside reminding people to give alms to help those in need, which is one of the tenets of Islam. Prasenjit has a funny bone and kept us in good humour during the two days that he was with us. I remember spending an evening with him by the river and exchanging information about our lives. COVID has changed many lives in Bangladesh too, and the loss of his father during the pandemic changed Prasenjit's life forever.

Hindus are a minority in Bangladesh, and any Hindu who realized I was one too, proclaimed their affiliation loudly and welcomed me in to see their community and their homes. One particular community at Vanghura Gram caught my attention and I happily spent close to an hour touring their homes, each a beautiful example of traditional construction that had undergone changes over time. Traditional foundations persisted, but mud walls and the thatch roofs had given way to tin sheets—as was the case in most of the homes from Bangaon on the Indian side of the border. I was told that the tin sheets had made an appearance during colonial times and had remained as they eliminated the need for regular maintenance. In this community, the kitchens stood out as separate standalone mud and bamboo structures with chimneys.

Another reminder of how these two countries had once been part of the same whole presented itself during our visit to the Chachra Shiva temple in Jessore. The temple reminded me of my earlier walk through Bishnupur in West Bengal. Built in the eighteenth century, the Chachra Shiva temple, a beautiful terracotta temple, has a two-tiered vaulted roof. The brick walls showcase intricate terracotta panels. The officiating priest at the temple welcomed us and said that we needed to maintain this gem for posterity.

It was heartening to see that most of the homes in the villages of Bangladesh still retained their traditional ways of building. They were built of wood and bamboo and were raised on stilts as waterbodies surrounded the home on some sides. These water bodies were a source of fish. The wetlands here were fertile ground; a poultry shed was built over the waterbody with a flooring of bamboo slats. The hen droppings became food for the fish. In the months when the water receded, paddy was planted, followed by jute.

As we neared Dhaka, in a place called Dohar, I started noticing sturdy and smart homes of wood, galvanized iron sheets with sloping roofs and trimmings that looked like wooden lace work. They looked rather out of place and I was brimming with curiosity. I stopped to chat. Mohammed Dipon had manufactured these knock-down homes that could be transported in parts and could be assembled at the buyer's site. The quality of the craft was superior, as was the wood. Dipon invited me in for a cup of tea and, as we chatted, he took out fine Dhaka cookies from his drawer and shared one with me. I felt it was something precious, meant only for special acquaintances, and as I munched on the delicious cookie, he popped the question—he wanted me to be his business partner across the border. I was stumped for a moment, and then I asked him to share his contact details with me so I could find him someone more suitable. I am still on the lookout.

As Dhaka came within sight—I had travelled two-thirds of the distance—things began to change. I mounted the pretty Madhumati bridge, the first six-lane Nielsen-Lohse arch-type bridge built in cooperation with the Japanese. Wide expressways gradually started replacing the narrow tree-lined avenues. We chose some detours through the villages to continue our tryst with nature and people as long as we could. Once we crossed Bhanga, we knew that we were in an urban territory. I tried many ways to secure permission to walk on the new Padma Bridge, but the government was firm that this bridge was strictly vehicular. Hence, I chose the ferry to get across these 6 km instead of taking a car across the bridge. The ferry ride was a memory to cherish. The Padma Bridge has changed things in more ways than we can imagine. Until then, Dhaka was linked to the south and south-west parts of Bangladesh only by ferry, and anyone wishing to travel there had to be prepared to either spare a few hours for the ferry or spend a whole lot of money for a flight. The journey takes less than 10 minutes now. The ferry ghats that earlier bustled with activity were now empty, and only a few boats were plying.

Many lives had been impacted as had livelihoods. We were fortunate to get a boat to ferry me across.

I reached the outskirts of Dhaka two days earlier than I had planned! I managed to get an appointment with Mr Pranay Kumar Verma, the Indian High Commissioner to Bangladesh, and it was a proud moment when I sat in his office to recount my experiences. He was inquisitive and had many questions for me, including ones that would help him get an insight into any travails that travellers could face.

This journey was different from the first walk in many ways. I was more relaxed for two reasons: I was familiar with what to expect, like it is with a second child, and moreover, I had planned this at a somewhat leisurely pace, to be able to enjoy the interactions without my body reminding me that it needed rest. This had been a shorter target and it came upon me before I even knew it.

Unity through design is particularly important for this region. Our countries are called 'developing nations' and we have held this tag for a long time. This tag itself rings of inferiority. Is that why we look elsewhere for inspiration and solutions instead of our own backyards? There is enough good work being done in our countries—of the place and for the place, for the people and of the people that they are being designed for. We need to grow these efforts, share and take inspiration from each other in this region and create our own vocabulary and we will soon be looked up to.

There is great power in the collective!

As I left the magic carpet of waterways, fields and trees behind me, my heart grew heavy. I knew that this exploration was ending.

I returned freer, surer and more hopeful of together being able to safeguard our actual wealth and our identity.

I will continue to walk—alone, together, for others, for change and to be changed.

My heart skipped a beat every morning,
as I saw the calm red sun rise—
a glow of promise,
a symbol of hope.

I marvelled at the magical tapestry,
an intricate weave of lush green and water—
lifeline or life itself?
Nature in fine balance!

The built was invisible as it sometimes should be,
a silent ode to all that is from earth
diligently playing its role—
ready to dissolve when its time is done.

What do I say of the simple folk?
The toothless grin and the sigh of disbelief.
A people of few possessions,
but rich in their love and generosity.

You say development will come.
I fear development will come.
And then what?
Will this too pass?

THE JOURNEY IS THE DESTINATION

The Buddha says, 'It is better to travel well than to arrive.' When I had hurt my foot in Gwalior and the completion of my plans was threatened, the essence of this saying gave me solace. I had travelled well thus far and I was definitely richer for the experience. I would certainly do what was required to finish what I had started, but at that moment of my injury, I chose to enjoy the breather that had come my way, even if it had not arrived in the most pleasant manner. I read. I spent time with people. I attended interaction sessions. I focused on healing. My cousin, a spiritual healer, Subba Vaidyanathan, sent me a recording for guided meditative healing. I practised that a couple of times a day. There were friends who practised long-distance Reiki and Pranic healing for me from wherever they were. I welcomed good vibes from any source.

I planned my options. Would I have to abandon completing the journey on foot? I had considered the option of enlisting the help of friends. There were 290 km left to reach the Delhi border. If each friend agreed to walk 5 km for the cause, I would have needed 58 such friends to complete the 1700. Many of my friends were athletic and could take on longer distances too. There could be a relay walk, which I was already planning in case I could not recover in time. I contemplated many such alternatives. I was rudely shocked when someone suggested that I walk only the last kilometre or when I neared places of interaction and the planned pause points, and quietly slip into the car in the interim.

'No one will know,' is what I was told.

'I would know,' was my gentle retort.

This initiative had not been planned to prove a point to anyone else. It was simply what it was: an honest attempt to explore our country from the lens of an architect and from the lens of the people that I met. Why did I need to use deception to achieve this goal?

I was exposed to gaps in our way of doing things daily, and these were added as summits to surmount on my future journeys. While I did feel despair when I observed these simple lacunae that could potentially become chasms, I also felt a sense of fulfilment at identifying objectives and goals that could lead me down different paths in the twilight of my life. There were questions staring me at my face that needed answers. There were problems that demanded solutions from our community. A diligent collation of stories and problems helped me narrow down our impact areas for the future.

Design Literacy

Making India design-literate is an onerous but much-needed task. Every human being is impacted by design almost every moment of their life, more so in today's times. This book that you are holding is also a result of many design inputs: the right size it needs to be for the hand to hold, the cover design to attract attention, the choice of font and the choice of paper are all design decisions. The apps we use, the hoardings we see, the tools we use—all aim to be designed for the best performance. There are specific designs to make life easier, like the Jaipur Foot, which has been designed to lessen the disadvantage that people who lose a lower limb face. The Liter of Light project is another such example of an affordable do-it-yourself lighting solution for dwellings without access to electricity.

Over 80 per cent of homes and small commercial establishments are built without the services of formal architects and designers. Many cannot afford the costs, others do not know of the existence of such services, and yet others do not appreciate the value that design could bring to their projects. The latter reasons make a good case for a movement on spreading design literacy. Design has enough power to enhance the well-being of the occupants of a home to ensure fewer visits to a doctor, lesser building and life-cycle costs, the power to harness renewable energy and hence, reduce dependencies on the grid. Design has the power to build mutual love, respect, empathy and belonging through the building of walls and even bridges. This awareness of the power of design needs to be taken to all.

Sumari from Namkum in Jharkhand opened my eyes to the passion that can move mountains to make even the most deprived individual realize their dreams. Until then, I had not imagined that someone from a remote location could love geography so much that they would be able to convey it through the twinkle in their eyes. This interaction reinforced my intent towards equipping students in high school with information on the profession of architecture to help them make considered choices.

If newer architects are passionate about the field, I can see magic happening. Our course titled 'Universe of Architecture' tells the story of architecture from the eyes of three children—each from the past, present and future. We translated this from English to Hindi and Bengali for my two walks and this, along with our presentation on design as a career, became part of my arsenal to build awareness on the power of design as I walked.

Making Design Accessible

Those who do not avail the services of an architect or designer often belong to sections of society for whom design is not a priority— hunger and earning a livelihood to make ends meet are. Professional services come with a price tag that they cannot even dream of meeting.

Traditionally, such professional services have seldom been availed. People built their homes themselves, and communities participated by giving advice and even contributing time, labour and resources. The community was equipped with the skills and the knowledge required to build a house and the system of mutual cooperation worked to ensure that homes were built. Changing times have led to the village inhabitants migrating to cities and the dynamics within village communities have been changed forever. The information and the ways of urban life have invaded the lives of rural folk and their aspirations have undergone a dramatic makeover. This difference is evident in every aspect of life, but the most visible differences, as always, are manifest in the newer buildings. All new building activity in villages largely mimics building activity in the cities, albeit at a very different scale and context. The activity of building has become a lot more complex. People who were experts at the traditional way of building are suddenly lost when they are building homes sans the courtyards and using newer materials and technologies. They could certainly do better with a little guidance and even guidelines. Just as there are doctors practising in government hospitals at the village level and health workers dispensing valuable advice on sanitation and well-being, it is imperative that local advisors are available to advise on construction techniques, local planning principles and materials.

Seeing Sumari's energy, I could sense the difference many such Sumaris from different parts of rural India could make to the regional identity if they chose to take up architecture for their careers. They know their context, they identify with their past, they understand their local social and cultural milieu and can understand the problems as well. They can continue to nurture the collective wisdom and can become the bedrock for creating and strengthening an evolving regional identity for the places that they belong to.

Universal Design and Accessibility

Design must work toward an equitable and inclusive society.

Observing the hardships faced by Harshvardhan Dubey of Datia, who is visually impaired, and revelling in the life story of Rani Mistry of Latehar highlighted existing social injustice.

In India, there are 26.8 million people who have disabilities, according to the 2011 census. But barrier-free movement is not yet fully supported by our public infrastructure. Many architects are also unfamiliar with the fundamental guidelines for universal accessibility, in addition to the general public, and hence, we do not see inclusive buildings and infrastructure around us. The population with disabilities is represented by 2.21 per cent.[36] Even though the percentage is lower

---

[36]'ADIP & RVY Joint Interface for Unique Nomination', *Department of Empowerment of Persons with Disabilities (Divyangjan), Ministry of Social Justice & Empowerment, Government of India*, https://adip.disabilityaffairs.gov.in/. Accessed on 23 November 2023.

statistically, the number, 26.8 million, is still high. The number of disabilities defined in the government guidelines have been increased since the 2011 census and hence these numbers would now be far higher.

We have 104 million older people (60+ years), constituting 8.6 per cent of the total population, an estimated 270 million pregnancies, and many more temporarily disabled by accidents. The particular needs of a pregnant woman, an old person, an adolescent, a child with a fractured foot, etc., are examples of people without permanent disabilities who would still benefit from a barrier-free world. That's why we call it universal design—a design that includes everyone!

The Preamble to the Convention on the Rights of Persons with Disabilities, adopted by the United Nations in 2006, describes disability by stating that: 'Disability results from the interaction between persons with impairments and attitudinal and environmental barriers that hinder their full and effective participation in society on an equal basis with others.'

Design can address inequities and it has the ability to play a huge role in blurring differences and empowering everyone equally.

The Hands That Build

As I ended the first day of my walk, I stopped at a construction site and slipped into a conversation with Bhola, a construction worker who was a part of the crew responsible for excavation and for filling the earth after the foundation had been laid on a site. I am an architect who engages with academics and with social causes. I am no longer involved in the actual design and construction of buildings. But it did come as a shock to me when I realized that Bhola was completely ignorant of what building was being constructed through his contribution. How would someone who does not know what is being created by the magic of his hands feel any affection for the creation, or even for the person who has designed the building? In fact, Bhola was not even aware of the existence of an architect. We often complain that architects do not get their due in society. Who is to blame if the very person who could be an ambassador for the architect is not aware of their existence? I began advocating that for every construction project, the promoter or the owner should maintain a log of every pair of hands that have helped in the realization of the structure. After all, at least a silent vote of thanks is in order. I also urge architects, promoters and builders to begin a project with a presentation of what has been conceived to the construction workforce.

Environment and Infrastructure

On the 1700, I saw roads of international standards and I would like to thank our country's planners for them. However, roads need to connect people, not divide them. Pedestrians, their routes, their needs and the local context should be primary drivers on highway and expressway projects.

While it appears to be a matter of time before most of these roads have public conveniences at regular intervals, the problem of adequate water supply often reared its head. Water was available for irrigation purposes but it was not potable in many places. Lack of water meant that the maintenance of toilets, wherever homes had them, was also a problem, and I saw many toilets that lay defunct. Community toilets are certainly a way out until the issue of water can be alleviated.

Enormous road surfaces mean a distinct rise in temperature and this has an impact on the environment. Large and well-planned plantations (even if they must be linear for want of space) alongside these roads and water catchment areas could make a huge difference. The choice of trees should be dictated by the local climate, soil condition and water table. I came across stretches where eucalyptus trees had been planted in drought-prone areas, which made the problem of water scarcity more dire. These issues need to be addressed as a part of the highway designing process and should be initiated alongside the execution of the highway projects.

Traditional Wisdom

I came across beautiful examples of self-designed spaces, homes and shops that constantly drove the point that people traditionally had an intrinsic flair for designing their own spaces and had a way with the craft of building and deploying different traditional materials and methods.

With time, the ways of building and preferences of materials have undergone a huge change. The choice of traditional materials or planning principles for new additions or new constructions is rather rare. In the quest to gain a sturdier roof over their heads and be rid of the stigmatic association of impermanence, a timeless way of building has been abandoned by many.

While we march ahead, our heritage is our wealth. The pace at which this change is happening is extremely rapid. We are in danger of being bankrupt of the immense knowledge only palpable in these structures of yore or the minds of our people. Efforts to document the mastery of these invisible monuments need to be taken on a war footing, on an exigent basis before it is lost forever.

And to conclude, as I often say to my team, 'There is no finishing line. The day I think I have reached or arrived at my life's goal will be my last. The destination may be the same for many but the journey to any destination is a personal one. That is yours and yours alone. I realized that it can be hugely empowering once you own your journey up to that fact. You have the choice to design that journey, to fill it with the tweeting of birds and the joy of being, to embellish it with the friendship of co-travellers or to travel a solo path, to lose your way and still find yourself in that loss.'

MY TEN COMMANDMENTS FOR REALIZING A QUEST

1. Allow it to completely possess you.
2. Write and clearly understand the reason for your quest. Have clarity on the intent and the outcome.
3. There is no alternative to planning. Attention to minute detail is a must.
4. Ask for and accept all the help you need.
5. Harness and utilize all the connections and goodwill you have built over time. Be unabashed about it.
6. Go to town with it, and the pressure will be on you. Pressure is the magic potion.
7. Yes, it will probably be the most intense and stressful time of your life. Learn to manage the pressures.
8. Read about other similar quests and learn from them. Reach out for advice from the achievers. Believe me, these large-hearted people will help.
9. Record the many magical moments of your mission of a lifetime. You need to see it as a mission to make it happen.
10. Enjoy the journey. The journey is the destination!

AFTERWORD

Raising awareness about the profession of architecture is at the core of the priorities of the Council of Architecture. As architects, it is our responsibility to take the lead in improving the quality of our built environment, thereby improving the quality of life.

We spend most of our time in enclosed spaces and these spaces become pivotal in shaping our personality, lifestyle, moods, productivity, creativity and well-being. The Council of Architecture is extremely committed to spreading this awareness and the 'Walk for Arcause' initiative fell in line with our primary intent. This is an innovative and rather unique initiative towards understanding the pulse of our nation, interacting closely with communities outside our own and spreading awareness about the role and power of our profession.

The Council is proud to have supported this mammoth endeavour and congratulates architect Gita Balakrishnan on the successful completion of not one but two such extensive journeys that have now blossomed into numerous well-informed initiatives touching lives through the power of design. The interactions and engagements along Gita's route have come as a great source of learning for us all. The information thrown open to us is enormous and will go a long way in helping us communicate with society at large.

We intend to make our profession and professionals more visible and emphasize how good architecture can make a difference in lives. This way we will create more work avenues for architects while helping the common people reap the benefits of engaging a certified professional for their design requirements, thereby moving a step closer towards a symbiotic relationship between people and their built environment.

With this in mind, the Council has always been associated and committed to what Gita coins as 'Arcause'—architects for a cause and for the cause of architects.

—Ar. Abhay Purohit
President, Council of Architecture

AFTERWORD

Dedicated to promoting excellence in architectural design and practice in India, the Indian Institute of Architects (IIA) joined the 'Walk for Arcause' campaign in partnership with the Ethos Foundation and the Council of Architecture. This endeavour aimed to raise awareness about the transformative potential of good design in improving lives. This was not a walk for one but a movement for the entire architecture and design community.

Gita traversed six states and the National Capital Territory on foot and our regional chapters along the route had the pleasure of walking alongside her at various stretches, interacting closely with communities and also partaking in initiatives that were born out of this expedition. The conversations revolved around the power of design, inclusivity, ensuring a barrier-free environment for all and exploring aspects of cultural sensibility, traditional wisdom, history, arts and crafts, geography, streetscapes and much more. The Jharkhand and Madhya Pradesh Chapters, covering longer stretches, organized multiple events and interactions, while a shorter segment in Haryana and Rajasthan also hosted a meaningful conversation. We walked, met, spoke, exchanged and explored more avenues of touching lives through design.

One of the most impactful outcomes has been the Universal Design Fellowship, for which the Jharkhand Chapter of our Institution partnered with the Ethos Foundation and School of Architecture, Carnegie Mellon University. Born out of our meeting at Deepshikha, an NGO working towards Child Development and Mental Health in Namkum, Ranchi, this Fellowship is currently underway as a humble first step towards raising awareness about diverse abilities and the need for a barrier-free world.

In addition, we are actively collaborating with other organizations and experts to initiate similar impactful projects, drawing upon the knowledge and insights our profession has provided us. IIA urges the leader in you to walk your mile by joining hands in this movement and contributing to the cause as this is just the beginning.

—Ar. Vilas Avachat
President, Indian Institute of Architects

ACKNOWLEDGEMENTS

A good idea planted at the right time becomes a magnet. It attracts all the goodwill and participation needed for its fulfilment. I am grateful each day for all the support I received to begin this mammoth endeavour and it endowed me with the confidence to make this dream of a lifetime come true.

My family has been extremely supportive—my husband has been a solid pillar of support—one that is central to this journey of mine. From the very inception of the idea to its acceptance, detailing, planning, execution and accompanying me on long stretches whenever he had the time, Bala was an inseparable part of this journey. Pranav, Gaurav and Shreya were totally with me in spirit through my highs and lows. As for my work family, the excitement within Ethos is hard to describe. Every team member dove in with enthusiasm to put together ideas to bring about a symphony that appealed to all and was meant for all.

I am indebted to Leander Paes for taking time to read the manuscript and for penning a thought-provoking foreword.

The idea of *Walk for Arcause* brought in its share of well-wishers—the Council of Architecture and The Indian Institute of Architects—who made this initiative their own and were an intrinsic part of the campaigns that were curated around it. I would like to make a special mention of the then President, Vice President and Registrar of the Council of Architecture, Ar. Habeeb Khan, Ar. Sapna Kumar and Mr R.K. Oberoi, respectively, as well as the current and then President of the Indian Institute of Architects, Ar. Vilas Avachat and Ar. C.R. Raju, respectively, along with the councils for the terms.

The Boston Architectural College and the National Association of Students of Architecture (India) along with the Indian National Trust for Art and Cultural Heritage (INTACH) joined the walk almost immediately after having received the request for partnership. The last two decades of Ethos have brought us different partners who value what we do and have invested in our efforts. We believed that it was important to invite all of them to be a part of this journey and that is how colleges of architecture and design, architecture firms and industry partners were walking with us. Generously supporting the walk and the cause, we had Saint-Gobain, Tata Tiscon, Kohler, ITC Vivel, Merino Laminates, Varmora Tiles, KLite, Tata Structura, Mahindra First Choice and TVS fuelling the initiative.

My interactions and the bonds I built were at the heart of this journey and kept me going through the toughest of days and have left me with a thirst for more. People who taught me just by opening up to me and sharing their stories are all a part of who I have become today. I still dream about the gleaming eyes of Sumari, who wanted to pursue a career in geography; Anjali, who enlightened me about the benefits of traditional building techniques while simultaneously expressing the need to move away from the same; Jagjiwan and Vidyapath, the two brothers who let me into their beautiful homes that they had crafted with traditional methods; Harshvardhan and Gopika, who taught me about the hopes and aspirations of people living with disabilities; all the children who floored me with their curiosity; and many more. Organizations and specialists working at the grassroots level towards the holistic welfare of vulnerable sections of society shared with me their learning and findings that have been critical in shaping the after-walk ripples. For this, I would like to thank the people behind the following organizations and initiatives—Mallabhum Prayas, ASHA, Deepshikha, Banwasi Seva Ashram, Jeevan Rekha Express, Art Ichol, PashooPakshee, TARAgram, Nirmana and Shri Vansh Gopal Lok Kalyan Samiti—for taking the time out to share their learnings and findings with me.

Health is the biggest parameter in the realization of such a quest. I am indebted to my doctors, physiotherapist, nutritionist and all the people I consulted with for confirming my ability to do this, brushing away my fears, sharing expert tips and being just a phone call away. Yes, a woman walking through highways and forests is not a common sight in our country. Many friends expressed their concerns about my safety. I am thankful to the regional police divisions for being available for any help. I laud my ground team, who supported the actualization of the walk and ensured all precious interactions were captured through photographs and videos for posterity.

This book has seen many hands and minds contributing to its realization. I thank Dibakar Ghosh from Rupa Publications for all the inspirational discussions that led to the making of this book and my editor Shatarupa Dhar, who transformed this manuscript into its final, polished form. I extend my appreciation to Rajkumari John, whose precision and artistry brought the words to life on the page, and to Swar Khosla for transforming my manuscript into a visual masterpiece with the cover design. Ar. Abhay Vinayak Purohit, the President of the Council of Architecture, deserves my gratitude for agreeing to spread information about this labour of love to colleges of architecture.

A special shout out to Rasya for bearing with my tantrums when the going got tough. I am deeply grateful to Shivani, Sejal and Krishna whose illustrations featured in this book breathed life into the route maps, and further enhanced the storytelling.

The ones who gave me the much-needed boost at the onset of my journey and to those who gathered to celebrate its accomplishment, I cannot thank them enough for making this a landmark event. Those who couldn't be there in person, yet joined me in not only spirit but also in action—through their own walks, activities and campaigns— have greatly contributed to enriching this initiative and making it a nationwide movement.

GRATITUDE WALL

Abhay
Abhijeet Baghel
Abhijit Singh
Abu Sayeed
Aditi
Ajay Dwivedi
Ajay Kumar Jaiswal
Ajay Mehta
Ahmed Nizam Mohaideen
Alamgir Kabir
Alok Sharma
Amandeep Jakhu IPS
Amit Baisnab
Amitava Ghosh
Anand Khatri
Annie Koshy
Anurag Garg
Anil Dewan
Anil Singh
Anirban Mukherjee
Anita Reddy
Anjali
Anjali Patil
Ankit
Anmol
Anshadha Singh
Anshuman Dewan
Anu Sogani
Anurag Kumar
Anurag Singh

Arijit
Arpana Kumari
Arvind Patel
Arvind Singh
Ashish Gupta
Ashok Das
Atul Saraf
Balaji Utla
Basant Kumar Madhav
Bhairavnath Pal
Bindu Naidu
Birendar
Biswajit Kalindi
Chandni
Chintamani Vishwakarma
Davinder Singh
Dharini Srinivasan
Dharmendra Gupta
Dhritiman Sarkar
Dilip Kumar Mahato
Dipsankar Mahata
D.P. Mishra
Erika
Father Alphonse
Geetika Agarwal
Gauri Shinde
Gaurav Agarwal
Gautam Bhandari
Gayatri Singh
Gopal

Gopika

Greeshma

Guddo

Harnarayan Rai

Harshvardhan Dubey

Hasibul Kabir

Heer Sharma

Hemant Malik and Alka

Ibrahim

Imrose Khan

Jagjiwan

Jaikeshav Mishra

Jashoda

Javed Miandad

Jitendra Mehta

K.P. Gorain

Kapoori Devi Yadav

Kaustav Das Gupta

Khushwant Sharma

Kiran Kapadia

Kirti Singh Baghel

Krishna Narayan Pandey

Lakhan Raja

Lakhan Srivastav

Lakhan Tehri

Lali

M.K. Sunil

Mahesh Daas

Maithili Jha IPS

Malay Ghosh

Maney Siby Ezhuparayil

Mangala Hareendran

Manish

Manjari Chakravarthy

Mansingh

Marina Tabassum

Mohit Kapoor

Mukul Goyal

NTPC Guest House

Nagendra Singh

Nalin Goel

Narendra Kumar Sharma

Navdeep Singh Gehlot

Neeta Awasthy

Nilmuni Murmu

Nirmal Makhija

Nishant Kathula

Panna Dutta Chowdhury

Parvati

Piyush

Prabhat Kumar

Pradeep Tiwai

Prakhar Agarwal

Pranjal

Prashant Das

Prashanta Naskar

Prem Chandavarkar

Puneet Sharma

Punit Sethi

Pukhraj Gaur

Pushkar

Rajesh Agarwal

Rajesh Bawri

Rajesh Chaudhary

Rajua

Rakesh Prasad

Ram Singh Yadav

Ramkrishna K

Ravi Sengar

Raviraj Parihar

Rekha Nemani

Rekha Taluja

Ripu Daman Singh
Rishu
Rupesh Shetty
S.R. Das
S. Selvamurugan IPS
Sabu Idicula
Saikat
Sakib
Sanchita Gupta
Sandeep Khirwar
Sandeep Kumar Jha
Sanjeev Bumb
Sanjiv Rangrass & Nalini
Satish Gupta
Satish Tyagi
Satyadev Prasad Agarwal
Saurabh Dixit
Selina Akter
Shahrear Rehman
Shalini Misra
Shantanu Chaudhary
Shashi Sharma
Shivani Goel
Shravan K
Simran
Smriti Mishra
Snehashish Bhattacharya
Soma Anil Mishra
Sourabh Sahu
Subhashish

Sudha Lhila
Sudhamoy Mondal
Sumari
Sundrarajan Muruganandhan
Sunil Maniramka
Sunita Devi
Surendra Baidya
Surendra Chaudari
Surendar Singh
Surya Kanta
SWAhealth
Thakur Prasad Rajak
Trambak Chakraborty
Tushar Sogani
Umang Sarawagi
Uttam Patel
Vaani Dua
Vaibhav Khare
Vansh Gopal
Varsha
Vijay Sharma
Vicky
Vidya and Madappa
Vidyapath
Vimal
Vinni
Vinod Mishra
Vinu Chaddha
Virendra Kumar
Vishnu Giri